PRESENTED TO:

_____

PRESENTED BY:

_____

DATE:

_____

101 THINGS YOU SHOULD DO BEFORE YOU RETIRE

DAVID BORDON AND TOM WINTERS

WARNER
Faith®

Project developed by Bordon Books, Tulsa, Oklahoma
Concept: David Bordon and Tom Winters
Project Writing: Vicki J. Kuyper, J. Heyward Rogers, and Lee Warren in association with SnapdragonGroup℠ Editorial Services

Warner Faith
Hachette Book Group USA
1271 Avenue of the Americas, New York, NY 10020
Visit our Web site at www.warnerfaith.com

Printed in the United States of America
First Edition: October 2006
10 9 8 7 6 5 4 3 2 1

ISBN:0-446-57920-3

LCCN: 2006921574

Introduction

Your retirement from the "official" workforce may be eminent or it may be a mile marker so distant that you can barely make it out from where you are now standing. Still, the experts would say that it's never too early to start planning and dreaming. In a very real sense, retirement is a journey rather than a destination.

Wherever you find yourself on the road of life, *101 Things You Should Do Before You Retire* was designed to help you get the most out of your journey, making important preparations along the way—and perhaps even giving you some fertile ideas you had not yet considered. We hope it will—at the very least—whet your whimsy, promote your life purposes, and give you food for thought as you travel. Bon voyage!

Years ago we discovered the exact point,
the dead center of middle age.
It occurs when you are too young to take up golf and
too old to rush up to the net.

FRANKLIN P. ADAMS

CONTENTS

*Our grand business in life is
not to see what lies dimly at a distance,
but to do what lies clearly at hand.*

THOMAS CARLYLE

101 THINGS YOU SHOULD DO BEFORE YOU RETIRE

1

JUMP-START
YOUR
SPIRITUAL
LIFE

G iven the pace of life during your peak working years, it's understandable that finding time to invest in spiritual things would be difficult. It isn't that your soul isn't longing for greater meaning and purpose; it's just that the tyranny of the urgent seems to always be in the way. Besides, that Bible looks so big and intimidating and time-intensive lying there. And prayer—you want to—but other things tend to take precedence.

It isn't easy—that's for sure—but it is possible to invest in a strong and vibrant spiritual life before you retire. The key is to find a workable plan that leaves little to chance. Simple Bible-reading plans are a wonderful solution. Some Bibles include them and many can even be downloaded from the Internet. Most plans are designed to cover only one or two chapters a day—in most cases that amounts to less than 10 minutes of reading time. Even if you cover just one chapter a day, you'll work your way through the entire Bible in less than three years.

Bible reading is a great way to invest in life after retirement, but it has very practical applications for life before retirement as well. Within its pages, you can learn how to handle conflict, manage people, live a life of integrity, and much more. The Bible also offers direction regarding prayer. It teaches how to relate to God, how to tap in to His wisdom and insight, and how to surrender your burdens and cares for a more peaceful life.

Don't let the daily hustle and bustle keep you from making your spiritual life a priority. It's the only investment you can make that extends into retirement and beyond to life after life, enriching and enlightening along the way.

2

MAKE
LASTING
FRIENDSHIPS
AT WORK

Remember that time Joe Cransky tripped over the projector cord and took a dive right in front of the entire sales staff? How about when Gordon Clemmons left his laptop computer sitting in the terminal in Boston? And who could forget when Luanne Kruger dropped a whole cheesecake in the elevator. Have you ever stopped to think about all the things you've shared with the people you work with? You've applauded their accomplishments and they yours. You've celebrated births and birthdays, spent untold hours talking shop, cleaned up after each other's mistakes, and even traveled together—sometimes extensively. But what will happen to those work relationships when you no longer see each other every day? Don't let those hard-won relationships languish when you retire. Start transforming them into friendships—now!

Begin by initiating contact outside the office. Come on—you can do it! Attend a ball game together, invite the whole family over for a cookout, exchange telephone numbers, ask about hobbies, interests, out-of-office activities. And when you're socializing away from the office, refuse to talk about work. You already know each other professionally. Explore who you are as people. Most of all, be up front with them about your motives. Chances are they'll be flattered to know that you want them to stay in your life for good.

The end of your work life doesn't have to mean the end of your relationships with people you have grown to care about. And it doesn't have to mark a solitary lifestyle. If you start now—before you retire—you can build strong, lasting friendships that will bless you for the rest of your life.

3

BUILD YOUR LIBRARY

Ever wish you had time to read those books everyone is talking about around the watercooler? And what about those books you enjoyed so much when you were young and carefree? The daily grind has a way of shoving time-intensive—though pleasurable—activities like reading right out the door. The good news is that it won't always be that way. In retirement, you'll be able to sit back and revel in the pleasure of a "great read."

In the meantime, don't let those hot titles get lost in the shuffle. Build your library now. It may not be as easy to come up with the cash later to purchase all the books you want. And some of the books you're interested in may slip off the radar before your feet are firmly planted in the grass next to your hammock.

When you hear about a book you'd love to read—Rebecca Wells' *Divine Secrets of the Ya Ya Sisterhood* or P. J. O'Rourke's *Age and Guile Beat Youth, Innocence, and a Bad Haircut*, for example—jot down the title in your daily planner and pick it up the next time you run errands. Or just allow your list to grow and then make periodic Saturday morning book runs. You can also order books online. Hello! Isn't that Amazon.com's whole reason for existing? Fill your virtual shopping cart with the books you would love to read, and when they arrive, put them on the shelf—with care—anticipating every moment of delayed gratification.

When you make an effort to prepare for retirement—mentally, emotionally, and spiritually, as well as financially—it will seem less like a black hole at the end of your career and more like a bright and promising reward for a job well done. Buying some books to read later can do all that? Sure it can!

4

PLAN A TRIP
DOWN
ROUTE 66

A day here, a week there—vacations can almost be more trouble than they're worth. Just about the time you start to relax and enjoy yourself, it's time to pack up and go back to work. But that will change one day. You'll pack up your desk, thank your coworkers for the nice retirement party, turn over your keys, and begin your "permanent" vacation. At last, time to do what you want to do—like taking a long, leisurely drive down America's historic highway.

The old Route 66 begins in Chicago, ends on the Santa Monica Pier in Los Angeles, and includes the mountains of New Mexico, the plains of Oklahoma and Kansas, and historic cities such as St. Louis, Tulsa, Amarillo, and Flagstaff. The Mother Road crosses eight states and three time zones. If you feature yourself to be a true adventurer, you might want to make a marathon drive taking in all 2,448 miles. If not, you can choose a stretch of particular interest.

You can drive only parts of Route 66 these days. It has been replaced by the interstate highways I-55, I-44, I-40, I-15, and I-10. A surprising amount of the original two-lane highway is still drivable, however, if you're man or woman enough for a real ride!

You can access all the information you need to plan the perfect Route 66 road trip at www.route66.com. It could be awhile before you are actually free to hit the road, but it's never too early to plan the road trip of a lifetime or take a few shorter drives down the Mother Road just for practice.

Retirement can be a tough transition—leaving the daily routines, familiar faces, and work-related obligations behind. But it affords many benefits as well. Time to get out and explore God's beautiful world is one of them. Start putting together your dream trip today.

5

SAVE, SAVE, SAVE—MONEY, THAT IS

E xperts say that you need to save at least one million dollars during your working years to sustain yourself in retirement. ONE MILLION DOLLARS! Are you kidding? Sounds like a lot, doesn't it? But that's about what it will take to maintain a decent lifestyle, cover rising medical costs, retirement housing, nursing care, and leave something for the kids. You haven't forgotten about the kids, have you? They're probably sitting around talking about it right now! And then, of course, there are the things you want to do—such as travel, entertain, and treat yourself.

Given that, it only makes sense to save as much as you can during your peak earning years. Any good financial planner can help you establish a system for socking away cash to be used and enjoyed later. Your tax specialist can help you take advantage of some pretty good tax incentives as well. Keep in mind that you don't have to be a high roller to plan for a better retirement. No matter how much or how little you have, you can always squirrel away some acorns to ensure your optimal comfort during the winter of your life.

The Bible has quite a bit to say about stewardship, but some people think stewardship is all about giving away money. Though charitable giving is an important element, stewardship also means making the best use of what you have been given. Saving rather than spending is a good way to start. Do your best to ensure that you will not become a burden to your loved ones or be forced to spend your golden years restrained by financial shortfalls.

Realistically, you may not need a million dollars to cover your retirement expenses, but be assured that whatever you put aside will be a blessing when the other income streams run dry.

6

THROW, THROW, THROW—STUFF, THAT IS

Do you keep adjusting your glasses because it seems the rooms of your house are getting smaller? Have you recently added a shed for additional storage? Has it been years since you could park your car in the garage? If your answer to any of these questions is yes, you are more typical than you might think. It seems that most people tend to accumulate more and more stuff as they grow older. And in many cases, it's not useful stuff—it's junk!

This is not about sentimental things that carry cherished memories of loved ones or friends. But you might be surprised to find that much of your storage space is taken up by broken appliances, left-over rolls of ancient wallpaper, and that cowboy boot lamp your Aunt Maddie gave you for the Christmas of '82. You might also find your closets stuffed full of clothes you won't wear again in this life—unless you wake up some morning a size 2 or corduroys come back in fashion.

The best way to end the madness is not to add to it. Don't bring home anything you won't use right away. Then set a time—say, Saturday morning—to start tossing things off the ark. Begin with one room, one closet, one drawer. No need to hurry. Even if you get to only one drawer or a closet a month, you're doing fine. Have a box for trash, a box for charity, a box for your children, and leave only those things you most cherish.

Gaining control of your stuff before you retire will make a big difference after you retire, whatever your plans—whether that means moving to a smaller house or entertaining more. Retirement is about maximum flexibility. Don't let your stuff limit yours.

7

PUT A MATCH
TO THE
MORTGAGE

One thing you should not carry with you into retirement is your home mortgage. If you play your cards right, you can put a match to your mortgage on or before your retirement party. Talk about free at last!

With a little prudent planning, however, you may be able to pay it off even sooner. Wouldn't that be great? Check the terms of your mortgage, and most lending institutions don't have a problem with it. One way to make an early payoff is by doubling up on your payments. You'll want to make sure, though, that the extra payment is going toward your principal balance rather than interest. You can find amortization calculators online to help you determine your payoff date or an advisor at your financial institution can assist you.

Rather than making additional mortgage payments, some people prefer to sell their large homes and use the equity to pay for a smaller home with less maintenance. Once the kids are gone, you may not need all that space anyway. A smaller home has lower utility bills and just seems cozier.

Retirement should be a time for maximizing your income and enjoying a little of what you've worked so hard for. A large mortgage—once your primary income stream has dried up—can only create stress and tie you down.

Make plans now to put a match to your mortgage on or before your anticipated retirement age. (Of course, when you try this, it's advisable to be in the company of a trained fire professional or at the very least have a fire extinguisher nearby!) It won't always be easy, but isn't it a delicious thought—spending your retirement years home free?

8

WHERE
THERE'S A
WILL THERE'S
A WAY

Last Will

~((and))~

When your children were small, you could always motivate them with the old parental standby, "That's it; I'm selling you to the circus!" But that is pretty lame when it comes to adult children—so most parents fall back on the ever popular, "That's it; you're out of the will." Except for billionaires, that cheap threat usually falls on deaf ears as well. But maybe it nudges something in your noggin that says, "Hey, what about that will?"

An amazing number of people never make a will, and without one, government red tape could eat up almost everything you have. What a waste of your time and hard-earned money.

An equally large number of people do make a will but leave it languishing in some drawer somewhere, slowly becoming less and less reflective of their wants and needs. The truth is that it's financially sound to update your will at least every five years.

Creating a will can be a chance to review your assets and refigure your net worth. It can also be an opportunity to turn assets into heirlooms. A list of your family treasures with the heirs' names next to them has two benefits. First, it prevents hard feelings and possibly even fistfights after you're gone. Second, it allows you to enjoy the giving of those gifts long before your will is read. Tell your granddaughter—while you're rocking her—"Granny's rocking chair will be yours one day. Someday you will be rocking your own granddaughter in this very chair." What a wealth of sweet memories.

So, don't put it off one day longer. Make that call to your attorney. And, who knows, just hearing you've updated the will may be enough to give you some clout with your grown kids.

9

⌘

TRY
THAI FOOD
. . . OR INDIAN
. . . OR KOREAN

Y ou might know people who are "pattern people." You might even be one yourself. Pattern people are quite comfortable with routines. In fact, if you take them out of their routines, they become irritable and out of sorts. But once in a while, when they are forced to try something new, they actually enjoy it— whether it's a new type of food, or drink, or genre of music.

To a degree, we are all pattern people. We all have routines. But even the most pattern-oriented person will admit that sometimes routines can lead to staleness. No matter where you are on the spectrum of extremes, make a point to try different types of food. What's the worst that can happen? You won't like it, and you'll leave hungry? That's why you have all of those deli meats stored in your refrigerator, right?

How about inviting a group of friends to a month's worth of Friday-night food nights? You can either meet in different ethnic restaurants or take turns gathering at each home with each host cooking a different style of food. If the night doesn't work out as planned, you can always order a couple of pizzas and consider it your Italian night!

Get into the habit of experiencing life and all it has to offer to its fullest. Don't wait for some distant time in the future when you'll start trying new restaurants or new anything. Experiment and take a few risks now, and enter retirement experiencing the joy of knowing that you already know what living life to its fullest feels like.

10

TAKE
POSSESSION
OF YOUR
DREAM RIDE

Y ou've been thinking about it for as long as you can remember. It drifts into your consciousness each time you park your minivan in the garage or make the monthly payment on your sensible work car. You watch the "vroom, vroom" commercials on television and slowly prowl the aisles at car shows. It's out there—waiting. It's the car of your dreams.

Your car may be a brand-new "in" car or a tried-and-true classic such as a Corvette or Mustang. Maybe when you close your eyes, you can see the gleaming metal of the stick shift or feel the wind in your hair as you glide along in the leather-seated luxury of a sporty convertible. You know what you want. It's your dream after all.

As you anticipate retirement, it's time to start hotly anticipating your new ride, as well. Become an after-hours shopper at car lots, check out the new models on the Internet, join a classic car club, or just read, read, read until you know all there is to know about your car of choice. Then, let the hunt begin.

If you're looking for a classic, let a couple of dealers know specifically what you're interested in. Check out sites such as www.collectorcartraderonline.com or www.cars-on-line.com. If it's a new car you desire, your best bet are car shows and new-car lots, where you have an opportunity to take a test drive.

The most important factor of all, however, is this: do not settle for anything less than your dream car. Absolutely refuse to get practical or tight-fisted. This car is your prize. You earned it. Keep looking until you find exactly what you're looking for—the car you can't live without.

11

GET YOUR CHOPPERS AND BLINKERS CHECKED OUT

E

F
P
T O
L P E D
P E C F D
E D F C Z P
F E L O P Z D
D E F P O T E C
L E F O D P C T
T C E O

Most people take it for granted that they will lose at least some of their hearing, eyesight, and maybe even their teeth as they grow older. That is so wrong. With just a little extra care and attention, it's possible to see, hear, and chew well into old age. So plan now for your best possible situation as your retirement years approach.

Okay, it's a pain to floss regularly and get regular dental, eye, and hearing tests. But think about what you are actually protecting: Your granddaughter's soft voice. Your ability to finish off a delicious steak. Your ability to read a menu, a good novel, or a love note from your spouse.

Even if your faculties are far from perfect now, you can still do a lot to preserve what you have. Be sure to have your eyes checked twice a year, wear sunglasses when you are out in the sun (Did you know it's possible to sunburn your eyes?), add the eye-strengthening supplement lutein to your vitamin regimen. Brush and floss after each meal. See your dentist often. Don't grind your teeth. Use your teeth only for what they were designed for—never use them to pull the cap off a pen or a bottle. Be realistic and aware concerning your hearing. Have your hearing checked at least once a year—no fudging. Keep everything out of your ears. Always have a pair of earplugs in your purse or wallet. Be careful with headphones and loud music.

It really is possible to reach retirement with your eyes, ears, and teeth in good shape and ready to serve you for many more years. If you treat them right now, they'll be there for you later.

12

DON'T
COME IN
OUT OF THE
RAIN

C. S. Lewis wrote of a friend named Jenkin, who "seemed able to enjoy everything; even ugliness." Jenkin had a peculiar practice. On a windy day, he sought out the windiest ridge from which to experience the blowing of the wind. On a rainy day, he found "the most dismal and dripping wood." He was determined to embrace all of life's experiences as they were offered up to him. He understood that there were more important things in life than comfort, more worthwhile endeavors than self-protection.

There's a certain wisdom in that view of life. But it's not the view of life that prevails in this society. It's amazing how insulated you can be from the outside world if you choose to be. Everything seems to be individually packaged, shrink-wrapped, and sealed for your protection. More and more, human experience and interaction are mediated through television screens or computer screens. It's not so unusual for a person to go for days without setting foot on grass or dirt without seeing the sky except through a window.

Are you one of those people who drives straight from the covering of your garage at home to a covered garage at the office? Would it really hurt you to feel a few raindrops on your head? You know the old saying: "He doesn't even have sense enough to come in out of the rain." But is it possible that you've been in out of the rain for too long?

Sometimes the sensible thing is to step out into the elements and get a taste of the world as it really is. And if you don't do it now, you'll find it even more difficult after you retire. Next time it rains, put away your umbrella, step out under the open sky, and don't come in out of the rain.

13

BECOME AN
EDITORIAL-
PAGE FANATIC

Y ou may—as many people do—have a tendency to flip past the opinion/editorial page of the local newspaper. During your busy work years, it's hard to find time to care about the nitty-gritty of grassroots activism and local politics. But the time is coming when you'll be in position to take a greater interest, perhaps even make a contribution to democracy in its most basic form.

For now, you can prepare by reading through the op/ed page as often as you can. It won't be long before you begin to recognize names and feel a growing fervor for local issues. By the time your days of perpetual sunshine (retirement!) arrive, you'll be a player, confident about where your skills and experience can do the most good.

For example, you might use your organizational skills to promote a neighborhood watch program or push for the cleanup of contaminated local sites. You could speak up for the preservation of a historical building, funding for a much-needed park, or the installation of traffic signals to offset a dangerous intersection.

You may want to speak out in the political arena by endorsing a certain candidate for office who shares your views on impending legislation. Our communities need to hear the opinions of cogent, faith-filled men and women.

Retirement is a time of rich opportunity—a time for giving back to the community where you raised your kids, earned a living, enjoyed the benefits so many others fought for and obtained on behalf of all your town's citizens. Soon it will be your turn. Thank the good Lord for the chance to make a difference in your world.

14

RECONNECT WITH OLD FRIENDS

Do you ever see an old photograph and think: *Whatever happened to Frank or Jolene or Luke "the Duke" or "What's her name"?* You think about all the good times you had together before life got in the way. No wonder some people say, "By the time I had time to enjoy my old friends, they'd moved away and left no forwarding address!"

Don't let that be your mantra in retirement. Put on your private-eye hat and start tracking down those old buddies now. You may not find them all, but even if you find a few, you'll be glad you made the effort. People change, so their responses may be disappointing, but most people would be flattered to know that you went out of your way to find them and rekindle the flame of friendship.

Modern technology makes that easier than ever. Directory assistance may be all you need—it's much more comprehensive and user friendly these days—but if that fails, almost anyone can be located through the Internet. Other good sources are your alumni directory and mutual friends.

Once you've found them—don't let them go. Call again . . . and again. Send a card, write a letter, send an e-mail—anything to breathe new life into the relationship. Plan a get-together to get caught up. Recall old times. After all, you've got nothing to lose.

Friends are important in every phase of life, but particularly in retirement, when you have a lot more time to hang out together and relax. So go ahead and reconnect. Odds are, you'll wonder why you didn't do it sooner.

15

❧

BECOME
THE FAMILY
SCRIBE

An unfortunate consequence of our fast-paced, mobile society is that families are often separated by thousands of miles. That makes it difficult to share the day-to-day joys and angst of each others' lives. But even when a job, the military, education opportunities, or some other circumstance takes your loved ones far from home, they are never really out of your reach.

Writing a family newsletter or manning a Web site are wonderful ways to stay in touch—and if no one else volunteers to take on the responsibility, how about taking the reins yourself. You're not a writer? Not computer savvy? No problem.

Most word-processing programs have built-in newsletter templates. If you're too unskilled to do it yourself, wait until a more technologically astute family member—the really good ones are typically between the ages of seven and ten years of age—comes to visit and get some help. Once you've found a template and design you like, you're in business. Send out a note to family members asking them to write up their news and send it your way. Then just paste their contributions into your letter. They do all the work—you get all the credit. Life is good!

You might also want to look into a family Web site. Several hosts offer free services, and many others offer hosting services for a nominal annual fee. Your site can be protected by a password so that only those in your family have access. You can post the photos from Cousin Bill's Louisiana coon hunt, share Grandma Benton's banana bread recipe, maintain a family directory of birthday and anniversary dates, update addresses and phone numbers—not to mention posting sinister notes to your cousin Glenda for running off with your best Tupperware.

Don't wait until you retire to enjoy your family. They are a gift to you from God. Grab hold of every precious moment you can.

16

⌘

REVISE YOUR LIST OF DAILY "DO'S"

Your work life may be great, or it may be a disaster. If it's anything, odds are, it's consistent. Same start and knock-off time each day. Same office surroundings—desk, fax machine, water cooler. Same tasks to be accomplished—budgets, phone calls, meetings. Yawn! And yet, in a perverse kind of way, there is comfort in knowing what you need to do each day, having a routine, understanding what is expected of you. Even if you think you would never miss it, you may find that you miss daily do's when they are no more. After all, they bring structure to your life.

Why not start a list of things you need to do every day after you retire—five is a good place to start. Don't try to plan your whole day, just a few things you can call routines. You'll want to give it some serious thought and include whimsical and spiritual items along with the practical. Maybe you'd like to spend more time in prayer every day, tend the yard, or cultivate a new hobby. Knitting, anyone? Have you thought about resurrecting those canvases and water colors? What about an exercise program?

You might find that some of your favorite things—activities you've put on the back burner during these busy work years—can become daily delights after retirement. Even if that's twenty years away, it could be fun just thinking about it. It could also be fun to resurrect and renew supplies for some of your bygone interests.

Routine gives a sense of purpose to life. Too many retirees find themselves feeling useless and unproductive. Make sure your retirement years are filled with interesting and life-giving daily pursuits.

17

VOLUNTEER FOR A TASK AT WORK YOU MIGHT ACTUALLY ENJOY

S ay—just for the sake of discussion—that you have a bit of extra time at work with which you could take up the slack for one of your coworkers or volunteer to manage one of the endless list of tasks that constantly needs doing. Which one would you choose? Instead of being satisfied to be the only one who can unjam the printer or bring reindeer cookies for the Christmas party, how about putting some thought into doing something different—something you might actually enjoy.

Take a look at the list—real or virtual—of the things you could volunteer to do. If you don't see anything of interest, get creative. Are you a photography buff away from work? Volunteer to take pictures at the next office party and give everyone prints. Are you known for your world-class salsa? Skip the cookies and bring your specialty to the next office party. This isn't so much about trying new things as it is about spreading your wings at work. It really is a good thing for others to know more about you and your interests and talents. They may all be surprised when you volunteer your band to provide the music for the company luau, but they'll get a kick out of it—guaranteed.

No two people are the same—even identical twins are not completely alike. God's given each of us gifts and talents with which to serve and bless others. Until the day when you close your office door for the last time, be sure to use your gifts on behalf of those you work with. It will make for a happier workplace all around and volunteering will be a joy rather than a drudgery

18

TWO
WORDS—*TIME*
CAPSULE

C lose your eyes and imagine the wonder of it. Your grandchildren and great-grandchildren, maybe even great-greatgrandchildren, stand staring into a treasure box—filled with the history of their family, engaging memorabilia, and expressions of love—that has made its way down through the years. Then look into the faces of those who have gone before—aware of significant similarities in the eyes, the bone structure—and marvel. Teenaged Jeffrey is excited to learn that someone else—Uncle Winslaus—also played the bagpipes. Cousin Jennifer learns that her beloved oyster dressing recipe came from her great-grandmother Robinson. What fun!

You are the one who can give them that gift. It won't take much effort. It won't be expensive. It won't tax your intellectual abilities or your physical dexterity. And yet, it's a gift that is priceless.

Pause for a moment and think about what you would like to know about your own ancestors. You would probably like to see what they looked like, know what they did for a living, find out about their gifts and talents, and see what their lives were like on a daily basis. And you might care to know if they loved and served God. So fill your time capsule, perhaps a shoe box or some other container that you resolve to be opened sometime in the future, with those things that give your loved ones a peek into your life and the lives of those who will one day be their ancestors.

Also include interesting information about the times in which you live. Comment on those things that are going on in the world. Everyone knows about World War II, but it comes alive when you hear it described by a veteran. Give your own grandchildren and greatgrandchildren a view of the world from your perspective. It's a gift that keeps on giving—now, later, and much, much later!

19

TRAVEL NOW— ON THE COMPANY NICKEL

H ave you always wanted to see a bit of Chicago, Los Angeles, New York, Philadelphia, or Houston? Maybe you've been wondering about a lot of locations outside the city limits of your hometown, but vacations are generally reserved for visiting your wife's sister in Poughkeepsie or your husband's brother in Fort Wayne. Besides who has money for such outings?

If that's the case, you might be overlooking the obvious—short trips at company expense. If you've never been invited along to visit a client or buyer or attend a conference, for heaven sake, volunteer. The worst that can happen is the boss says "no"—and your attendance might even provide a welcome break for some road-weary business traveler.

Even though business travel is designed to get you in and out quickly, there are things you can do to get the most from the experience. Consider taking a couple of vacation days and bookending them around the business portion of the trip. Two days in Orlando before driving up to Panama City for a day or two of meetings. Two days in San Francisco after the trade show is finally over.

Instead of just meeting for lunch at the most convenient place, think about treating your client to a business lunch in a restaurant with lots of local flavor. Or better yet, ask your client about the local attractions and suggest you meet at one of them. The client just may have as much fun as you do. And nothing beats bonding over a good time. You can bet that the client won't soon forget your visit.

Your work life doesn't have to be a series of long, uneventful days. By the time you retire and are free to choose your own travel destinations, you can be seasoned—an accomplished tourist, with trendy luggage and digital camera in tow.

20

LEAVE A LEGACY

How would you like to be remembered by your coworkers? The office prankster, the delicate flower who couldn't take criticism, the whiner, the preacher, the obstruction-ist, the person who's never wrong? Or maybe you'd prefer: "Remember Harry? One time he painted the whole lunchroom by himself on a weekend. What a guy!" or "Susan had a way of making people feel good about themselves—even when they disagreed with her."

The closer you get to retirement, the less control you will have over how others will remember you—your legacy—so act now. Start becoming the person you want others to remember as an inspira-tion, a positive influence. Begin by taking a good hard look at your attitude toward your job. If you don't take pride in what you're doing, chances are you're not striving to do it well. Work is more than something to pay the bills and pass the time until retirement. What you do matters. Every job, even a menial one, is part of a big-ger picture that keeps society functioning. Look at each task in light of the big picture. Then give it all you've got. Leave a legacy of excellence—even in the little things.

When it comes to your coworkers, leave a legacy of love. Next to your family, your coworkers are probably those you spend the most time with. You may be as close-knit as a wool ski sweater—or you may have to contend with company politics, abrasive personalities, or unfair practices. Only you can choose how you will respond. Becoming the person you want to be isn't always easy. But it's worth the effort. Leaving a legacy of excellence and love is a nice way to be remembered, but more importantly, it gives you a past you can reminisce about without regrets.

21

TURN THE
RETIREMENT
TIMETABLE
UPSIDE DOWN

Between our many aches and pains, the viewing of mortality tables with our insurance representatives, and the constant reminders we hear to "get your affairs in order," it's no wonder so many people are afraid of retirement, viewing it as that period of our lives when we are obliged to sit in a rocking chair on the front porch and wait for the end to come. How ridiculous! Retirement might be one of the later stages of life, but it certainly need not be the last.

In the Bible, there's the story about a man named Abram. When he was ninety-nine years old, God appeared to him and told him that by the following year, he and his eighty-nine-year-old wife, Sarai, would have a son. How's that for a retirement package? The story goes that Abram literally fell to the ground laughing. Sarai laughed too when she heard it. But in spite of their laughter, God did just what He said He would do, and a son that they later named Isaac was born the following year.

You're probably laughing right now too, wondering where this little history lesson might be going. Well, it's just an example of the fact that age or stage of life is absolutely no obstacle for God. Even if you are currently engaged in a life that is full of meaning and purpose, His primary plan may not yet have been revealed. Could be there's a writer, an artist, a poet, a volunteer, a world-changer inside you still waiting for a chance to express himself or herself.

No matter how far you are from retirement, let God inspire you to look toward the future with a heart of adventure. Laugh if you want, but don't underestimate what God has planned for your golden years.

22

SHOW THOSE YOUNG WHIPPER-SNAPPERS A THING OR TWO

No matter how far along your career path you are, there will always be a few ambitious younger types who think they know it all. Children of the information age, they have answers for everything—though little experience to back them up. They walk around flaunting their high-tech gadgets—palm pilots, BlackBerrys, text messengers, pocket PCs—while you may have to make do with what's in your head. How are you supposed to keep up?

Easy. The closer you get to retirement the more good old-fashioned practical experience you have to offer. After all, it's easy to collect data, but it takes experience to know what to do with it. So don't stress out over all those young whippersnappers. They don't yet know what they don't yet know. Instead of becoming frustrated and insecure, make nice. Ask one of them to teach you how to access your e-mail from your cell phone or download music files. Chances are your actions will amount to an equalizer, allowing them to interpret your gesture as a sign of acceptance and an invitation to relax and get to know you as a person. Oh sure, you might learn that there is at least one uptight, overwrought youngster in the bunch—but you're mature. You can deal with that.

The workplace doesn't have to be a standoff between the younger and older employees. It takes only one person—and that person can be you—to guide the others toward a team environment that pays big benefits for all involved.

Instead of throwing down the gauntlet and calling for a duel, use your weaknesses to foster peace and your maturity to develop a complementary workplace. You might even learn how to program the iPod your teenager gave you for Christmas!

23

〜◦⟡◦〜

SAY "HI" TO THREE STRANGERS EVERY DAY

Remember when people used to sit on their front porches and greet those who passed by—strangers and friends alike? Weren't those the good old days? Okay, fine—so you aren't that old. But maybe you've read about how it used to be before people started huddling indoors in front of the television set, driving directly into and out of their garages, and keeping to themselves. We now live in an isolated society where it is possible to live next door to people you have never met or spoken to.

Your best protection against isolation and loneliness both now and in retirement (you won't even be going out to work) is to develop an attitude of openness—even with strangers. Of course, it may not be wise to approach perfect strangers in our dangerous world, but every day you probably encounter a host of familiar strangers: the checker at the grocery store, the UPS man who delivers packages to your office, the order-taker in the sandwich shop down the street, and many more. Why be shy? Saying "hello" with a warm smile does not amount to inviting them for Christmas dinner.

This simple exercise will put you in the practice of reaching out, creating an attitude of accessibility. By the time you lock your office door for the last time and head home, you'll be a practiced greeter—someone who is much more apt to make new friends and establish postretirement relationships.

The truth is that you'll be helping others as well. Lonely people are everywhere. You might be surprised if you knew. But since they don't wear signs, the loneliest people are often right there among us. Your warm "hello" could mean a positive human connection for someone who desperately needs it and an investment in your own future happiness.

24

BECOME A
DABBLER

You may be an avid hobbyist—someone who knows exactly what you like—but most people aren't. Most people go to work each day, come home to their families in the evening, pay their taxes, and try to keep up with their lives. It's a fact of life. But one of the perks of retirement is the ability to focus on something outside the scope of responsibility, something that gets your motor running and your blood pumping.

Finding that special something can spell fun for you now if you're willing to indulge in a little dabbling. You can get started by making a list of ten things you find fascinating. Don't worry if you know next to nothing about those things. You may find yourself drawn to figure skating though you've never donned a pair of skates. Or you may love art though you've never studied it or tried it yourself. The point is to dabble in a lot of things you are interested in to find that one thing you can really go crazy about.

Once you've made your list, begin your research. Look on the Internet, or check out some books at the library. If your enthusiasm starts to ebb as you dig deeper, drop it and move on. You're looking for a pastime that really sustains your interest. When you've made your eliminations, give each idea a little try. Find someone with some experience to take you on a beginner rock-climbing outing, visit an auction with someone who knows his way around, or put on some skates and see how you do at an indoor rink. Many cities have them.

Doing a little dabbling can help you find a hobby that will bring you great pleasure even before you retire. And once you have some well-earned time on your hands, you can really invest yourself in it!

25

STAGE A

REVOLUTION

Remember when you were young and idealistic? You probably believed that you could change the world. Perhaps you spoke passionately about causes you believed in, and you were optimistic about your chances of success. The world just needed a little coaxing. But as the years went by, you realized that the world is a much bigger place than you imagined—full of people who hold opposing views. Thus, you may have settled into a routine lifestyle and concerned yourself only with the challenges of everyday life.

If that sounds like you, it's time to yank yourself up and shake yourself around. It's time to reclaim your passion, refocus yourself mentally, and go back to the business of world changing. Sure it's daunting, seems impossible. But you've got more going for you than you had back in your younger days. You're wiser, more experienced, less likely to be overwhelmed by unexpected challenges.

Start simply by doing something, anything—big or small—that has the potential to make a difference in even one life. By now, you probably realize that changing one life changes the world as a whole. So choose something you care about, and make it a place to begin.

No matter what you settle on, a group probably already exists—from politics, to taking care of the environment, to literacy, there are plenty of choices. Find a group who advocates a position you believe in and enter in.

Jesus once said that the kingdom of God is like a mustard seed—the smallest of all seeds. It eventually produces a plant that is larger than all the other plants in the garden. So don't worry about the size of your contribution—just do what you can and expect God to make it count. By the time you reach retirement, you'll be in the habit of changing the world.

26

❦

DREAM OUT LOUD—WITH A FRIEND!

D reams aren't as socially acceptable as one approaches retirement age as they are for younger folks. The closer you get to retirement, the more people expect you to be established, content, and thinking about slowing down. Any hint of wanting to start a new business, or buying a new sports car, or desiring to write a novel is frowned upon. Some call it an identity crisis. Others call it a sign of immaturity.

Either case could be true if we're out of balance. But the truth is, all of us dream, and most of us are afraid to tell others about it for fear of being judged, or worse—laughed at.

Does your best friend know what you dream about? If not, then it's time to tell them! The next time you are together, get a little philosophical. Ask your friend about his or her dream if you don't already know what it is. If you do, then bring it up and ask specific questions about it. Then talk about your own dreams and have fun discussing all of the "what ifs" with each other.

A conversation such as that might just give one or both of you the courage to pursue your dream. The Bible says that hope deferred makes the heart sick. No matter how old you are, don't keep your hopes and dreams to yourself. Dreams aren't just for the young. Keep yours alive long into your retirement years by nurturing them over a good cup of coffee with a close friend and allow the hope you receive to spur you on.

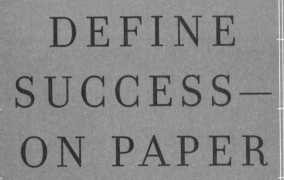

27

DEFINE SUCCESS— ON PAPER

Most of us chase some form of success our entire lives. But like a dog chasing his tail, we spin in circles because we never stop long enough to define success. It's just an abstract goal in our minds that we hope to achieve without ever actually knowing what it looks like.

Take thirty minutes to write down your definition of success. Be specific, but don't worry about your definition being perfect. You can always go back and revise it. In fact, if you struggle through this exercise the first time, it might help you to see that you are a little off course. That's okay. There's still time to right the ship. Just keep working on the definition until you have it right.

By taking the time to put your definition on paper, you'll solidify it in your mind. Transfer the definition to your Daytimer or to a 3 x 5 card that you can carry with you in your wallet or purse. And the next time you feel as if you are drifting through your life without any real purpose, refer to it.

If you do have an idea about what success looks like in your life, does it line up with how the Bible defines success? In the book of Luke, Jesus quoted Moses from the book of Deuteronomy when He said that we are to worship the Lord and serve only Him. How does serving God enter into your definition of success?

When you define what success means to you, you'll have an added sense of purpose and momentum when you reach your retirement years because you will have spent your working years pursuing the right path.

28

REACH OUT
TO THE
"ALREADY
RETIRED"

A bsolutely without a doubt the best way to anticipate the challenges and benefits of retirement is by seeking out the "already retired." These people have had an opportunity to review their preretirement choices in the light of postretirement realities. They've discovered any mistakes they may have made in their calculations regarding housing, finances, hobbies, health, or any other topic pertinent to living a happy, carefree postretirement life.

Uncle Louie can tell you right away whether giving up the five-bedroom house where he and Aunt Alice raised their nine children and moving into a condo in a retirement community was the right move, and if not, why. Your friend Wes who retired last year should be able to tell you how it's working out now that he no longer has a regular paycheck. Is his financial planning proving to be sufficient? Is Social Security adequate to meet the needs of your older cousin Kevin? What adjustments did Uncle Gene and Aunt Grace have to make in their lives? How are the friendships holding up? Is much more time together proving to be a good or bad thing for their marriage?

Those who have gone before you can be your best resource for peeking beyond the postretirement curtain and seeing your future. And the best part of this arrangement is that the already retired are usually eager to share the good, the bad, and the ugly with you—often without even being asked. All you have to do is hang out and let them know you're there to hear how things are going. Everybody wins.

29

BECOME A "BOOK-CLUB GROUPIE"

D o you ever feel that people just don't have the time or desire to engage in discussions about things that matter? You may be right. Most people find themselves so strapped for time that they can ill afford lengthy talks about anything, especially if it isn't an issue that directly impacts their lives.

Years ago, people had time to share meals, play cards or board games—and they had time to talk. But for the most part, our culture moved away from those types of social events a long time ago. Still, there are places where stimulating conversation can be found. One of those places is a book club. Just look to your nearest bookstore or library where book clubs abound in just about every area of interest you can imagine.

Book clubs discuss characters' motivations, actions, and thought processes. Questions such as, "Was the protagonist really so lonely that he was willing to go that far to try to find a friend?" often lead directly into discussions about real-life experiences and issues. Book clubs are also a great opportunity to meet people who—like you—enjoy and appreciate the honest exchange of ideas and opinions.

In the Bible, the apostle Paul told us to encourage one another (see Hebrews 10:25) and to build each other up (see 1 Thessalonians 5:11). Book clubs give you a great opportunity to do both. And becoming a book-club groupie will also give you the incentive you need to start reading again. You won't necessarily enjoy every book you read for group discussion, but you will be expanding your horizons, sharing your thoughts with others, and making new friends. And as you close in on retirement, that expanded social network could mean more and more to you.

30

CLOSE
THE DOOR
ON DEBT

Albert Einstein called compound interest the eighth wonder of the world. Think about it: a thousand dollars put out at 8 percent yields a mere eighty dollars in the first year—not especially impressive. But if you leave that money alone for nine years, that little 8 percent, compounded, has doubled your money— two thousand dollars. Leave it alone for another nine years, and it doubles again: four thousand dollars for doing nothing! Yes, that is a wonder. Compound interest is like a lever, translating a little bit of effort on one end into big results on the other end.

But have you ever thought about what compounding means when you're a borrower instead of an investor? When you owe money, you are on the wrong end of the lever. The borrower, you might say, gets the short end of the stick. The same principle that grows your money effortlessly when you're investing makes it that much harder to catch up when you're in debt. That's why it's so important to close the door on debt now, while you have more financial flexibility, instead of after retirement.

One great resource is Larry Burkett's book *Debt-Free Living: How to Get Out of Debt and Stay Out,* available at www.amazon.com.

According to the book of Proverbs, "the borrower is servant to the lender" (22:7). When you owe a debt, another person—probably a person you've never even met—has a claim on you. Now is the time to set yourself free. If there is any way you can get out of debt before you retire, by all means do it. And just as important, get out of the habit of taking on more debt. Why spend your retirement years on the wrong end of the lever?

31

BECOME A
MOVIE
AFICIONADO

Movies—long, epic tearjerkers and fast, action-packed thrillers. What fun! But who can afford to spend two hours sitting in the theater. Certainly not a working stiff who comes in tired at night and spends the weekends doing yard work and cleaning out the garage. Movies are something we dream about doing when we get the time—one of those postretirement leisure activities. Only problem with that strategy is that you miss so much in the meantime and realistically, by the time you have the time, you may not have the money. Have you seen the price of a movie theater ticket lately?

Fortunately, technology affords us a host of reasonably priced options to the cost and time it takes to see a movie in the theater. Of course, the movie rental industry is not new, but advances in technology have made them increasingly appealing. DVDs and other advancements have improved the quality of the picture significantly, and one company even offers rentals by mail. If you don't have a card, it's time to get on board. And the traditional movie rental is hardly your only option. Cable television now provides a wide assortment of movies, even new releases.

So, you might be asking, "What's the big deal about movies?" Consider this: movies can be a great form of relaxation, entertainment, education, and social input as you glimpse into the lives of people in unusual situations and unusual places. Don't wait. Become a movie buff now. You may have to limit your indulgence now, but one day you'll be in a position to really enjoy yourself. How great that will be!

32

❧

START
PUTTING
TOGETHER A
WORK HISTORY

We spend many hours every week doing our jobs. Over a period of years, imagine how much of our lives that adds up to. Don't let it float away with time—create an interactive work history.

Begin by buying a scrapbook and creating a section for every job you've had—at least those you can recall. Even if you're still a long way from retirement, you might be surprised to realize how many jobs you've had. Begin each section with the stats: a brief description of the job, the date when you began and the date when you moved on, where the job was located, how old you were, why you took the job, what you learned, what you liked, what you didn't, whether it influenced your later job choices. Then fill up the rest of the sections with memories of coworkers, significant events, old photos. You could even include the salaries you were paid if you want to give your grandchildren a good laugh. Eighteen thousand dollars a year was once a fairly decent salary for upper management!

Your children and grandchildren may see your project as mildly interesting at first. But when they begin to encounter challenges in their own careers, your work history could be a great encouragement. Seeing that you had missteps, experienced being laid off, spent time in jobs you hated and jobs you loved, got stuck in positions without the chance of advancement—all could help them deal with similar issues. They might also be encouraged by your achievements and urged to new heights in their own lives.

So get started. At the very least, you'll have a fantastic memory book that you will enjoy for years to come.

33

START A
BUSINESS

Be honest now. Have you had an idea floating around in your head for years? Maybe it's an improvement you've come up with for an existing product or service. Maybe it's a unique idea you haven't seen in the marketplace. Whatever it is, you may not have felt you could realistically pursue it because of family responsibilities, financial concerns, or time limitations. Could be it's time to take your big idea down off the shelf, dust it off, and see what you can make of it.

As you approach retirement, you are looking at an excellent time to pursue your dream. Wouldn't it feel great to put all the business savvy you've acquired through the years to work on your own behalf? The children will be gone, your work days free, and your finances somewhat secure. What could be better?

Begin by getting your idea down on paper. Regardless of the size of your endeavor—anything from raising and marketing free-range chickens to refining, packaging, and selling Aunt Gertie's fruitcake recipe—you will need a clear and concise understanding of what you hope to accomplish.

Enhance your idea statement with a vision statement and then move on to a lengthy list of pros and cons. Why do you think your idea will work? To whom do you plan to market your product? Where will you keep your inventory? How will you distribute it? What skill level will be necessary for those who perform the service you offer? These questions will later make up your business plan.

You may not have a lot of time to devote to your business pursuit, but this prep work will enliven your passion and help you develop your idea in an organized, responsible manner. Someday you could be the CEO of your own business. It's something to think about.

34

PICK YOUR
PARADISE

I t's time for an internal art project. The good news is that means it doesn't involve pipe cleaners or a glue gun. All it takes is an active imagination. So, get warmed up. Do a few mental calisthenics. Then, begin to paint your own portrait of paradise.

It may include palm trees—or a log cabin in the woods. How about snow-capped mountains, pounding waves, or a desert sunset? Take a good look at the picture you're constructing. Does it remind you of somewhere you've visited or is it simply a composite of some of your favorite landscapes?

Next, imagine actually living in this personal paradise. How does the landscape change? Does it need a mall? A golf course? Karaoke? Your grandkids? If you're married, you may want to involve your spouse in painting a picture of paradise together. After all, this project can be a lot more than mental gymnastics. The opportunity to pick your paradise actually lies ahead of you during the retirement years. Of course finances are a part of the picture as well. But for right now, simply dare to dream. Then, look at how your financial picture can frame, in a practical way, the place you have in your head.

If you've ever dreamed of living in a land where you don't have to shovel snow or where you can hear coyotes howling at night instead of sirens screaming down the highway, begin to consider how you can make your dream a reality. Research communities that have the topography, weather, and amenities your paradise entails. If you have a little vacation time, check out a few of these places firsthand. Who knows? Your own private paradise may have a mailbox with your name on it.

35

INCREASE
YOUR
PASSION
FOR PRAYER

You may have memorized prayers as a child and recited them for a Sunday school teacher or your parents. And maybe there was a time in your young life when you transitioned from scripted prayers to heartfelt prayers and you just knew that God heard you. You believed that He listened earnestly to those who speak with Him in faith.

But it could be that you have never felt a true passion for prayer. You've never experienced the excitement and inspiration of setting goals in prayer, seeing yourself as a person in league with God to change things in the world for good. If so, you are on the periphery of one of the greatest adventures on earth.

Prayer is more than hoping and wishing. It's developing a working relationship with the God of the universe. Imagine being a player in the building of God's kingdom or fulfilling His eternal purposes. This is the best apprentice program of all—an opportunity Donald Trump and Martha Stewart clearly cannot offer.

The way to begin is to begin. Ask God to open your eyes to the needs around you. Then ask Him for wisdom in how to pray. If that sounds circular, it is. It is God's way of involving you in His affairs.

When you discover a need, write it in a notebook with a date. Then talk to God about the situation often and openly. Do more than simply repeating the words over and over. You aren't talking to a statue that cannot hear you. Speak to Him as you would a caring Father, an almighty Creator, an unfailing Friend.

Your prayer passion is bound to follow you wherever you go— into retirement and out the other side, all the way to eternity.

36

❧

DEVELOP A
RETIREMENT
INCOME
PLAN

Retirement is going to be, as they say, "Way fun!" But the amount of actual fun you have has a great deal to do with cold, hard cash. Better to come up with a plan now—while you're still able to leap tall buildings with a single bound!

First, you need to figure out what you already have. Begin by checking the statement you receive each year from the Social Security Administration. It contains the amount of Social Security you have earned and what you can expect to receive, depending upon the age at which you choose to retire. Then determine how much will be coming in each month from pensions, 401Ks, annuities, or any other investments you've made. You can call your financial representative, and he or she will help you determine a total approximate monthly benefit based on your current investment plan.

If the picture doesn't look too bright, there are things you can do. Start putting the maximum amount of before-tax income into your retirement account, develop a skill you can work at part-time after retirement, and move some of your investments from conservative to more aggressive stocks, for example.

Saving for retirement, however, should not become an obsession. When God blesses you financially, He means for you to be prudent with what you've been given, but He also intends for you to be happy, to enjoy the hard-earned fruit of your labor. So enjoy what you have, share what you can, and put some aside for retirement. It's a policy that will keep you smiling through all the seasons of your life.

37

THANK
SOMEONE
WHO HELPED
YOU IN YOUR
CAREER

Do you remember the turning point in your career—that moment when everything fell into place after you received the break or the promotion that set you on the path you followed to where you are today? Your break or promotion probably happened because somebody took the time to help you in some fashion by explaining the intricacies of your line of work or by showing you his or her secrets of success—or maybe someone put in a good word for you.

Have you ever gone back and thanked that person for what he or she did? There's a story in the Bible about ten lepers who went to Jesus and asked for healing. He told them to go to the priest, and as they were going, they were healed. Only one of the ten went back to thank Jesus.

We can't be quick to condemn the other nine though, can we? We are often too slow to thank others for what they've done for us. Don't let this opportunity to thank somebody who has helped you in your career pass you by. Call or e-mail the person and offer to take him or her out for a meal where you can offer your heartfelt thanks. Maybe you could even buy the person a small gift to show your appreciation.

If more than one person has helped you, by all means find a way to thank all of them. But do it now and enter your retirement years feeling good about the fact that you let people know how much you appreciated their help.

38

~~~~~~

THINK
YOUNG

We've all heard, and probably repeated, the old saying, "You're only as old as you think you are." None of us really believes that we can stay twenty-one if we just think like a twenty-one-year-old, but we've all seen people who, as they age, slow down simply because they feel that they are supposed to.

You hear them say things such as, "Forty-year-olds aren't supposed to be playing softball or flag football" or the more generic, but popular, "I'm too old for that!" When people begin to believe they are too old for something, they modify their actions, and their bodies adjust accordingly.

Don't let that happen to you. A proverb in the Bible says that as a man thinks in his heart, so is he (see Proverbs 23:7 KJV). Think young, and your overall mood and health will probably benefit as a result. The next time someone invites you to a company or church picnic where activities such as volleyball or nature walks are going to be involved, jump at the chance. The next time you catch yourself going home early from an event just because you "should," catch yourself and resist the urge. Just enjoy the moment.

You probably can't do as much as you once did, but it might surprise you to know how much you really can do. Remember how Grandma Pearl or your great-uncle Herb never slowed down a day in their lives? Let that be a lesson to you. Think young and you can enter your retirement years as one of those retirees whom people look at and wonder, *Where does all that energy come from?*

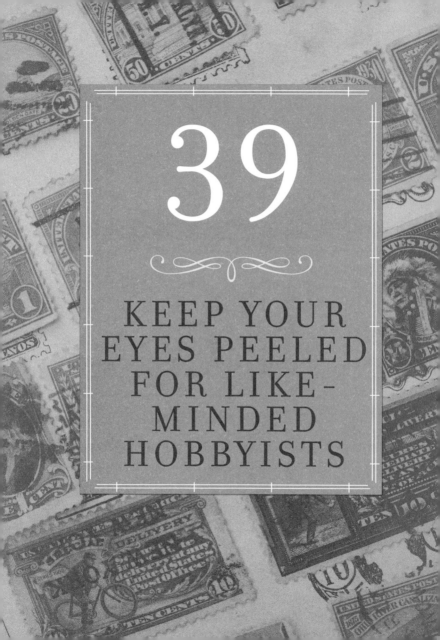

39

KEEP YOUR EYES PEELED FOR LIKE-MINDED HOBBYISTS

Hobbies are a lot more fun when you share them with others. Passion and enthusiasm grow exponentially in a group—even if that's just a group of two or three. All the more reason to seek out people who share your love of books, horseback riding, car shows, needlepoint, rock climbing, anything that piques your interest.

Of course, finding others who share your hobby will have practical advantages as well. You may find they are a sensational resource for helping you find rare pieces for a collection, historical information for a project, or help learning a particular skill.

The greatest perk, however, is that your hobby has helped you develop friendships—the kind that won't go away when you leave your place of employment or move to another part of town or even lose your spouse. Join a group of stamp collectors, and you've got a peer group for life. Members will move in and out, but the group will accommodate those changes.

So how do you go about finding like-minded hobbyists? Look in the phone book for clubs, ask at your local library, search the Internet. Go to the place where you purchase your hobby supplies and look for a bulletin board. If you love kite flying, spend time in the park. If your thing is airplanes, go to nearby air shows and don't just stand around—strike up conversations.

Resist the temptation to think of your hobby as a waste of time and money—something that should not be pursued until retirement. Hobbies provide inspiration, lifelong learning, skill development, social interaction, relaxation, and a lot of good, old-fashioned fun. It could help you live longer, and it's certain to help you enjoy your life more.

40

RECONNECT
WITH
ROMANCE

Remember what you felt like when you first realized that you and your spouse were going to be spending the rest of your lives together? You had a clean slate, a fresh start—a whole lifetime of togetherness stretched out before you. If you were like most young couples, you were just giddy with love. Over the years of your marriage, that giddiness has probably evened out, and that's probably a good thing. But every now and then, don't you miss the romance of young love?

You're coming up on a whole new phase of life. Hopefully, you're going to be seeing a lot more of your spouse after you retire. You've got a clean slate, a fresh start; and just as when you first got married, the rest of your life—a life of togetherness—stretches out before you. Don't forget: you have one major advantage over the younger you, however—you and your spouse already know one another inside and out. The giddiness of young love has matured into something deeper and more stable.

Maybe you and your spouse don't feel all that romantic any-more. That doesn't mean you can't find romance again. This is one area of life that's definitely worth the trouble. Schedule a regular date night. Light a few candles at dinner. Play the music you danced to when you first fell in love. See if you can find the DVD of the first movie you went to when you started dating. Leave notes on the bathroom mirror or slip a love note into the morning paper. You've got the rest of your life to look forward to. Now is the time to reconnect with romance.

41

ESTABLISH
A HEALTHY
EATING
LIFESTYLE

The family calendar that hangs on your refrigerator some-times seems to run your life rather than the other way around. And in between all of those events you are racing to attend, you probably grab food from wherever you can find it. You have to admit that you don't always make the healthiest choices, right? Eating a big greasy burger almost seems like a reward for enduring our hectic lives.

But that mentality leads to poor health, and given the positive changes in menus that you can find at almost every restaurant— including fast-food places—it is time to establish a healthy eating lifestyle. Hey, if Jerrod from the Subway commercials can do it, you can, too!

If you don't know where to start, just pick up a nutrition pam-phlet that most restaurants now have available and scan it for the foods that they highlight as the healthiest. Or visit the restaurant's Web site in advance and look over their healthiest choices. Com-panies such as Weight Watchers and E-Diets have Web sites set up to not only educate you about how to eat healthy, but to help you track your healthy eating.

Just get started. Even if you start out with the wrong method, you'll quickly realize it and move on to the next until you find one that works for you—and that's the key. When you find healthy foods that you actu-ally enjoy eating, you're much more likely to eat better food.

Your body will thank you as you head into retirement because you'll feel better. And while there aren't any guarantees, you'll have done your part to avoid surgeries for clogged arteries and various other ailments—and that means a happier, healthier, and maybe longer retirement for you.

42

❧⟶◦⟵❧

REFUSE TO
LET FEAR
HIDE IN THE
SHADOWS

F ear can be debilitating in life. Not because you can't beat it, but because if you don't try, it can steal your good times and wrap you in a blanket of powerlessness and failure. The way to beat fear is to face it head-on rather than allowing it to lurk in the shadows.

One wise person has suggested that the answer to overcoming fear is to do the very thing you fear most. That means, first and foremost, dragging it out into the middle of the room and taking a good hard look at it. Oddly enough, that is sometimes enough. Some fears are so irrational that they cannot stand the light of day. Other fears may be tougher, but they, too, can be vanquished.

Perhaps your fear has been standing up to your boss—asking for a raise or demanding credit for your work. You may have visualized a nasty confrontation that ends with early, unplanned, nonnegotiable retirement, and you were letting fear silence you. It's also possible that the boss will turn you down—but at least you will have submitted your request to a person, rather than to your idea of the worst-case scenario. Regardless of his or her answer, your boss may well gain respect for you just for asking.

Maybe your fear is flying, speaking in public, standing up to your mother-in-law. Whatever it is—do it! According to 2 Timothy 1:7, God hasn't given you a spirit of fear. What He has given you is a spirit of power, love, and a sound mind. He's given you the tools you need to overcome.

Enter your retirement years with the exhilarating knowledge and freedom that comes from knowing that you were able to look your biggest fear in the face and send it packing. Don't allow anything to keep you from enjoying your life to the fullest.

43

WALK,
WALK,
WALK!

S omewhere along the way, most of us developed an all-or-nothing attitude about physical activity. If we aren't able to run up and down the basketball court or dive on sand volleyball courts, then we often opt for a sedentary lifestyle. But the choices in life are rarely all-or-nothing. Most of us live somewhere in between.

Walking fits well into the in-between scenario. That's the very reason you might be surprised to learn that walking is considered by experts to be the very best exercise you can do, regardless of your age. It deftly promotes cardiovascular health, proper circulation, weight control, and strong motor skills. Getting out and about even stimulates your brain. Walking is an exercise that will keep you strong and vital long into your retirement years.

There are a number of options that can help you "get into" walking. Think of it as a sport. Power walking is popular with people of all ages. Wear proper shoes, and walk on a track when you can for maximum ease on the ankles and knees.

If power walking isn't for you, try hooking up with a friend. A stimulating conversation and a few good laughs can make your walking more enjoyable and keep you motivated. It's difficult to blow off your regimen when someone is waiting for you at the curb.

Other options abound. Try walking at the mall, walking with a Walkman, or walking a nature trail. Some people take along a cassette tape for the purpose of learning another language during their walking time or listening to a lecture or notes from a business meeting. Read Leslie Sansone's best-selling book *Eat Smart, Walk Strong.*

44

HIT THE ROAD IN AN RV

So you've been thinking about buying an RV and hitting the open road the week after you retire. You love the idea of traveling without having to fork over big bucks for hotels each night while having all of the amenities of a hotel. But not all RVs are created equal, and just how exactly does a person go about not only finding RV camps to stop in each night, but finding the best deals possible? Don't fear, RV clubs are here—and everywhere else, too.

Take some time to peruse RV clubs online. One neat Web site that lists many such clubs is www.rv-clubs.us. Various clubs offer discounts on things like camping fees, electrical hookups, water usage, and entertainment activities like the use of hot tubs and tennis/basketball courts. Some even offer free magazines to members.

Before choosing a club, make sure you compare features and also make sure that the camps they offer discounts for are predominant throughout the areas of the country where you plan to travel. Many clubs have maps on their Web site that will show you where each participating camp is located. And you'll also find specific information on these Web sites that will answer "frequently asked questions," such as "How much does an average night cost?"

Above all else, have fun with the investigation process! Allow yourself to dream about the places you'll travel to. Think about smacking the tennis ball around with your spouse—or enjoying the hot tub with him or her.

Arming yourself with knowledge about RV clubs and allowing the anticipation to build as you head towards retirement will appease your fears of the unknown while at the same time tickle your sense of adventure.

45

ROUND UP
THE FAMILY

A baby sits on the knee of a ninety-year-old aunt—the family's past and its future connecting by a look and a touch. Two cousins reconnect after twenty years of living in two different time zones. An uncle regales you with stories of your grandmother that you have never heard before—stories that might have been lost forever if the two of you had not made the effort to sit down together.

Such moments between family members don't happen often enough in a world where everybody seems to be going in a hundred different directions at once. It's not that people don't want to get together with the family. It's just that life gets in the way. You know how it is. People move. They get busy. Life's pressures have a tendency to drive extended families apart unless somebody is intentional about keeping them together.

As retirement approaches, you begin to turn your attention away from daily urgencies toward those things that matter most. And what matters more than family? Maybe it's time you took the lead in making a family reunion happen. Send out a letter, e-mail, or fancy invitation, suggesting possible dates. Start a family e-letter asking for input. Or get on the phone. You know best how your family connects.

It doesn't have to be anything too elaborate, unless you want it to be. The important thing is to give the members of your extended family a reason to drop what they're doing and make the effort to get together. The joy of reconnecting with the people who mean the most to you is amplified by the joy of seeing them reconnect with one another.

46

BECOME A
BLOGGER

T he diary is making a major comeback—not on paper, but on the Internet in the form of Weblogs, or blogs for short. Literally millions of these online journals are floating around cyberspace, each providing a window into the life of the person who writes it. Some focus on specific topics—current events, a favorite sports team, a specific hobby or interest. Others are more free-floating, offering up a running record of the blogger's thoughts.

You've done some living. You've got something to say. A blog is a great way to express yourself, to put down your thoughts in a form that other people can read and relate to. Like any other kind of journaling, blogging gives structure to your thoughts through the discipline of writing: Sometimes you don't know what you think until you try to put it into words! But a blog has the added benefit of allowing you to share those thoughts with others who may be far away. Friends and family all over the world can read your blog and interact with you and with each other. What's more, people you've never met but who share your interests can find you and join in the conversation. It's not the best place to record your most private thoughts, but a blog is a great way to leave your footprint on the World Wide Web.

And it's easier than you think. A good (and free) place to start is www.blogger.com. By the time you retire, you'll be a veteran blogger with time to blog to your heart's content.

47

EXCITE
YOUR
BRAIN

You may feel like an old dog, but that doesn't mean you can't learn a few new tricks. The community colleges in your area offer a wide array of new things to learn and new experiences to enrich your life. Maybe you've got a creative urge. Art classes, photography classes, or writing classes could give you a whole new way to express yourself. Learn a new language in preparation for a trip to another country—or just to expand your horizons without leaving home. Take courses in the field you now wish had been your college major. Many community colleges offer outdoor living courses that culminate in great camping, hiking, or paddling trips. Most have their course offerings posted online—or you can go to the campus and pick up a paper version of the course catalog.

Then there's the social aspect of a new educational experience. Think how many friends you made when you were in school. Continuing education courses reopen that door to new friendships with people who might be quite different from you.

Keeping your mind active during your retirement years is as important as keeping your body active. Think how much stimulation you get every day at the office. Sure, you look forward to rest and relaxation—to a little less mental stimulation—but on the other hand, there's such a thing as too much relaxation. Classes at a community college are a great way to keep yourself moving and keep a foot in the larger world.

48

MARCH TO
YOUR OWN
BEAT

arly in life, we are taught that our duty is to conform to society's dictates in terms of education, career, and lifestyle. Most of us peek out from under the canvas of common thought from time to time. But, for the most part, we do what is expected of us. Nowhere is this more evident than in the company setting where employees are asked to fit in, avoid rocking the boat, put the best foot forward.

The thing is that at some point in each of our lives, we discover that there's an original beat deep down inside us—a beat that gets louder day after day. When we are marching to that beat—the one God has placed in us—we are our most creative, most whimsical, most productive self. Some companies have recognized this fact and capitalized on it—but sadly, most still want conformity to the company model. These are the lions of management who recite the worn phrase, "We've always done it this way."

If this has been your experience, conform no more. This isn't about flaunting company policy or stirring up trouble. But it is about deciding to listen to the beat within. Push innovation, think outside the box, plant the seeds of change, trust your unique ideas, and share them with your boss. Even if you are rebuffed, eventually, someone will listen.

It's too easy to see retirement simply as an opportunity to distance yourself from the parade—and what a waste that would be for you and for the company you've invested so many years in. March to your own beat, and you might be surprised who will follow.

49

CASH IN
YOUR
COUPONS

Used to be you had to be sixty-five or close to it before you could start taking advantage of senior citizen coupons, but times have changed to accommodate the baby-boomer generation. AARP discounts are now available at fifty-five, and more and more businesses are dropping their age requirements to fifty-five and sixty. That's right—senior coupons aren't just for the old and frail anymore.

These days senior discounts can be found in movie theaters, dry cleaners, restaurants, retail stores, hotels and motels, car rentals, vacation packages, and banks, to name just a few. Between discounts and coupons, you can save some serious cash, and you don't have to wait until retirement to do it.

Aging robs us of so many things—our svelte bodies, our athletic prowess, our youthful naiveté—so what's the sense of passing up a perfectly good perk? After all, you're not a novice. You've earned every advantage you can get along the way.

So keep your eyes peeled. Check out the windows of the businesses you frequent. Look for that little tag on the menu, the ad in the newspaper. Once you start watching for it, you'll be surprised how many businesses are competing for your patronage with good discounts and coupons. In fact, when you don't see a senior citizen discount advertised, ask for one. You never know when you might wake a business owner up to the benefits of courting the senior set.

All right now, get out there and buy—for less, of course!

50

PUT YOUR
FEET ON YOUR
DESK—JUST
THIS ONCE

How many years of hard driving has it been now? You didn't get where you are by putting your feet up on your desk and taking it easy. But now that retirement is near, have you considered putting your feet on your desk and taking it easy? Not all the time, mind you. You aren't retired yet, and you still have responsibilities. But it probably wouldn't hurt for you to kick back just this once—just for practice. It's time to start learning to relax.

There's more to life than work. If you don't know that already, you'd better learn it soon. Even at the office, there's more to life than work. And feet on a desk, hands behind your head is a good posture for contemplating those other things that constitute a life well lived. It's also a good posture from which to have a conversation—a real conversation, not a meeting or a brainstorming session—with a coworker. A coworker who, by the way, isn't just a coworker but also a fellow human being with hopes and dreams and difficulties. When was the last time you had a meaningful conversation while hunched over your desk, bearing down on the task at hand?

Of course, it wouldn't be a good idea to turn into a total slacker at this late stage in your career. There will be time enough for that after you retire. Nevertheless, it might be a good idea, just this once, to try slowing down a little and putting your career in perspective. You can hunch back over your desk later.

51

CAMP OUT
WITH YOUR
GRAND-
CHILDREN

A child's face aglow in the flickering light of a campfire. The white flag of a deer's tail disappearing into the deep green of the forest. Holding hands to hop rock to rock across a mountain stream. There is hardly any better way to make happy memories with your grandchildren than to take them camping. Isn't that why you want to retire someday—to have more time with those who mean the most to you? Why wait? By the time you retire, your grandchildren are apt to be full-fledged adults themselves. Catch the wave before it crests.

The world looks so different to your children than it did to you. Places that were farmland when you grew up are now sprawling suburbs choked with traffic. Your grandkids spend much of their time with devices that weren't even invented when you were their age. But a camping trip is like a trip back in time. The forests in your state parks look a lot like they looked when you were a child. And a conversation around a campfire—where no television or video games interrupt the chirping of the crickets—looks a lot like a conversation you might have had with your own grandparents when you were growing up. It may seem as if your grandchildren live in another world from the one you grew up in—but on a camping trip you can find common ground.

Your grandchildren may be begging you to take them to Disney World. That's fine, too, if you can swing it. But you'll make a lot more memories for your dollar in a tent or a camper.

52

REWRITE
THE
RULES—AT
HOME

As you know already, in order for a household to run smoothly, everybody in the house has to do his or her share. No doubt you and your spouse arrived at a workable division of labor long ago. Maybe, like many couples, you never really discussed it. Perhaps you just gradually and tacitly worked yourselves into a list of his jobs and her jobs around the house.

But that division of labor was probably based on the assumption that you would be at work five days a week. Is that same arrangement still going to be equitable and fair when you're no longer on the job? Suddenly your share of the household responsibilities may turn out to be far less than your spouse's share. If you aren't watchful, you may find yourselves in the middle of a conflict. Your spouse, after all, is probably looking forward to your retirement as a sort of retirement of his or her own—looking forward to having you around more to shoulder more of the load. Do your expectations match up in that regard? This is one of those things you need to be intentional about.

You might also want to suggest to your spouse that it could be fun to tackle jobs together—a dish-washing duet in the kitchen or a gardening duo. Such togetherness can be a pleasure for both you and your spouse.

Retirement is a new phase of life—a new season—and new rules apply (or need to be negotiated) in many spheres. The good news is that this new season isn't going to sneak up on you. Now is the time to talk to your spouse about how your roles and responsibilities will change after you stop punching the clock.

53

AMAZE YOURSELF
WITH YOUR
ACCOMPLISH-
MENTS

With head down over the mower, you go up a row, then down a row, up a row, then down a row. With each pass you're making only twenty-two inches of progress. It seems you'll never get done. But you keep pressing on—up a row, then down a row. It's a slow business. Take a step back, however, and you realize that you've made more progress than you thought. String together a few twenty-two-inch rows and a nicely mown yard starts to take shape.

Life can feel like that a lot of the time, especially when you're still in the middle of the rat race—up a row, then down a row, just plodding along, about twenty-two inches of progress at a time. Today probably doesn't feel so very different from yesterday. That's why it's so important to take a step back every now and then and see what all the plodding has added up to. Sit down and make a list of the things you've accomplished over the years. Reflect on how far you've come. And don't limit yourself to professional accomplishments. What kind of progress have you made in your personal life? What lives have you touched? How have you made your community a better place to live?

It will do you good to think about what you've accomplished. You might even find yourself freshly motivated and creatively challenged. No doubt you'll think of things that you wish were on your list of accomplishments but aren't. It's not too late to balance out your list. Your accomplishments should be a source of satisfaction. They should also be a starting point for the rest of your life.

54

TAKE A ONE-MONTH SABBATICAL— FOR PRACTICE

Retirement is one of those things that people dream about for decades. Everybody thinks they know how to take it easy. But when retirement time actually arrives, the reality of it can be a little scary. Are you really ready for such a big lifestyle change? A short sabbatical of a month or so may help you find out.

Perhaps you were planning to get a nice reimbursement check for all that personal leave you have piled up instead of using it before retirement. But it's possible that a short retirement simulation may be a better way to invest that asset. Take a month and try to live as if you're retired. You might discover, for instance, that you aren't ready to retire after all. Maybe you'll discover that you need more income than you thought you'd need after retirement. Maybe you'll decide you like it so much that you'll retire a little earlier than you had planned. In any case, taking a sabbatical now gives you a chance to get used to the idea of not going to the office every day; after so many years of hard work, relaxing may not come as naturally as you expect.

The idea behind this kind of sabbatical is to do the things you expect to be doing after you retire. It's not a true vacation—not a cruise or a trip to Europe (unless you plan to spend your retirement touring Europe or going on cruises). The point is to find out how a retirement routine suits you. It's hard to know unless you've tried it.

55

TRY A NEW HAIRSTYLE

air salons are always promising "a new you." In some ways, retirement is all about "a new you" too. The retired you will be quite different from the workforce you—not at the very core of your being, of course, but in some significant ways nevertheless. You'll have whole new ways of spending your time. You'll go different places. You may socialize with a different set of people than the people you socialize with now. Maybe the "new you" needs a new hairstyle.

There's something about a new hairstyle that helps to define a new phase of life. Every time you look in the mirror, you are reminded that there's something different about you. Sure, your hairstyle is a small thing—maybe even an insignificant thing. But sometimes it helps to have an outward sign of a new attitude, a new outlook on life.

You may be one of those people who are so set in their ways that a new hairstyle seems like a drastic step. If so, that's all the more reason to take the plunge and try wearing your hair shorter or longer or a different color. It's not like it's permanent. And it isn't nearly so drastic a step as retirement is going to be. That's the point, really. You're in for some big changes when you retire, and you'll have the chance to do a lot of things differently. A new hairstyle is one place to start getting used to the idea. And it's a whole lot less commitment than a tattoo!

So take a good look in the mirror, viewing yourself from different angles. Look around at the styles and cuts of those around you. You might even want to pick up a magazine on the topic. But whatever you do—get excited and get ready to turn a few heads.

56

STOP SKIMPING ON BEAUTY SLEEP

I t's called beauty sleep for a reason: You really do look better when you're rested. Sleep is one of the great miracles of the human experience. Not only does a good night's sleep improve the way you look, it also improves the way you look at everything else. You've experienced it yourself: worries that plague you by night melt away while you sleep, leaving you with a fresh new outlook in the morning. Or a problem that has not yielded to your most concentrated thinking and figuring somehow solves itself when you go to sleep and let your subconscious go to work on it. Sleep is a vital part of a life well lived. As you get more and more intentional about the way you structure your life, be sure plenty of sleep is part of the plan.

Sleep is how the human body restores and rejuvenates itself. It's a genuine human need—such as food or drink or shelter. Most adults need seven to nine hours of sleep every night. It's possible that your body needs less than seven hours, but do you ever feel sleepy during the day? Does fatigue ever make it hard to do the things you need to do every day? If so, you need more sleep.

After you retire, hopefully you'll have plenty of time to sleep. But there's no reason not to go ahead and start getting your full complement of beauty sleep now. Your busy schedule may make it seem that you can't afford a full night's sleep. The truth is, you can't afford not to get one.

57

TAKE A
PERSONAL
RETREAT—
PREFERABLY
OUTDOORS

T he battle is raging—hot and heavy. The military precision of the fighting men starts to dissolve among the chaos. Things look different on the ground than they did in the war room—the battle and the battle plan turn out not to be exactly the same thing. That's when the voices of the officers can be heard over the din of battle: "Retreat!"

It seems strange to say it, but one of the most important skills of a successful army is the ability to retreat. To retreat is not to give up the battle or admit defeat, but rather to withdraw long enough to regroup for another charge into the thick of things, stronger than ever. Retreating is an important skill in ordinary life too. You need to pull back every now and then and see the big picture that sometimes gets obscured when you're in the midst of everyday living and everyday relationships. You need a place to hide away, a place to retreat so you can regroup, rethink, and gather up your strength for another charge into the middle of things.

There are lots of ways to have your own personal retreat. Go fishing. Go for a hike. Hole up in a cabin somewhere. Your retreat doesn't have to be outdoors, but if it is, so much the better. There's something about being among trees and rocks or beside a body of water that refocuses your mind and heart on the things that are most important. The key is to get away from daily concerns and activities and from the people you see every day. Then, as Shakespeare's Henry V put it, "Once more into the breach!"

58

OUTLINE YOUR AUTO-BIOGRAPHY

Y ou've got a story to tell. You're the only person who has ever lived such a life as yours. Have you ever thought about writing down your story for others to read? An autobiography is a big project—maybe bigger than you feel like tackling. But an outline of your autobiography is a great way to dip your toe into the literary waters.

You might think your life hasn't been something that's worth writing about. Don't let that keep you from at least writing an outline of an autobiography. As you begin to write, you'll probably realize that there's more to your life than you thought. Start by thinking about how much things have changed during your lifetime. Then think how many things haven't changed at all. What are the chief life lessons you have learned, and how did you learn them? It won't be long before you'll see that there's plenty to tell about your life.

Maybe you have the opposite problem. Maybe you feel you have so much to say that you couldn't possibly get it all down. Outlining your story will help you to get it all organized into a manageable form. Once you've got an outline, maybe you'll be ready to jump in and start actually writing the story.

There's probably at least one person who would love to read your autobiography. What greater treasure for a loved one? But there's a lot of benefit to you as well—because as you sit down and think through your life so far and try to organize your experience into some coherent form, you will begin to see how you have become the person you now are. Your autobiography will not only help others understand who you are, it will also help you understand who you are.

59

ANTICIPATE
INTROSPECTION

S ocrates said the unexamined life was not worth living. But the workaday world isn't the best place for self-examination and introspection. There's always some fire to put out. There's always some emergency screaming out for attention, some water-cooler controversy, some intrigue of office politics to occupy your mind. Nobody's paying you, after all, to gaze at your navel and think deep thoughts. You're there to look outward, not inward—to take care of customers, make widgets, manage people, sell products, make little rocks out of big rocks.

But the time will come when all the customers and coworkers will be gone; you'll leave the making of widgets and selling of products to other people; all the fires and emergencies will be somebody else's problem. And you'll have a lot more time to think.

Maybe it's time you got reacquainted with yourself. Spend some time asking yourself life's deepest questions. What exactly is it that motivates you? How did you become the person you've become? What really matters to you the most? Does your life match up with the things you say you believe?

Introspection is a good thing, and it's almost inevitable that you'll be doing a lot more of it. In the absence of so many things that turn your attention outward, of course you're going to spend more time looking inward. You may remember things about yourself that you had forgotten. You may learn things about yourself that you never knew. Are you ready for the reexamined life?

60

SWAGGER OUT ONTO THE DANCE FLOOR

J ust because disco is dead, it doesn't mean that your dance days have to come to an end. Actually, this is the perfect time of life to head back out onto the dance floor. But before you break out that old leisure suit and strike a John Travolta pose, it may be time to polish up some of your dance moves.

Taking dance classes isn't only for those with two left feet. Today it's hip to take hip-hop and saucy to salsa. And don't forget the cha-cha, waltz, tango, polka, or good old-fashioned square dancing. There's a dance style for any mood you happen to be in. Though you'll find plenty of classes available at traditional dance studios, don't overlook inexpensive group sessions at community centers or line-dance lessons at venues that feature country music.

Plain and simple, dancing is fun. But it's also a great way to stay in shape throughout the coming years without having to don a pair of sweatpants. Although it will be nice wearing all those Hawaiian shirts once you retire, it's also nice to have an excuse to get all spruced up once in a while. Your spouse will thank you for it. He or she will also thank you for taking a few lessons so you can be light on your feet instead of constantly on your partner's. With a little practice you really can look—and feel—like the belle of the ball.

So, cast off those inhibitions from that prom fiasco thirty years ago and rediscover the joy of moving to the music. Who knows? You may find that your inner Fred Astaire or Ginger Rogers is just itching to cut a rug.

61

BECOME A
MENTOR
AT WORK

You probably remember what it's like to be young and new on your job. You never quite know where you stand. You do your best work, but you don't know if it's good enough—or, for that matter, whether anybody noticed. Talent and ability don't always translate directly into confidence—especially if you're a newbie. To a person in that position, a word or two of friendly encouragement goes a long way. Look for opportunities to speak a few uplifting words to a promising young person at work—it's no trouble to you, and it will do that person a world of good.

Maybe you're willing to go even a few steps farther to help someone else succeed. Have you considered taking a new employee under your wing and becoming a mentor? Smooth the path for a talented young person in your office by making your years of knowledge available to him or her. Perhaps you could save that person from making some of the same mistakes you made early in your career. Seeing a young colleague flourish under your leadership is a fulfilling way to cap off your professional career. What better way to leave a legacy in the industry you will someday retire from?

People look up to their older colleagues. You've been around the block—your opinion matters. A comment that seems small to you—whether it's a positive or a negative comment—can be a very significant moment in a younger colleague's life. Be an encourager at the office. It's a great way to finish well.

62

MAKE A HABIT OF SAYING "I LOVE YOU."

Preparing for retirement is all about establishing new habits. Why not get into the habit of expressing your love on a regular basis? Don't go to sleep at night without saying "I love you" to your spouse. Don't leave the house in the morning without saying it. Try ending every e-mail to a loved one, every telephone conversation, with the words "I love you." Draw your children onto your lap and tell them how much they mean to you. Write letters and notes, send cards. Resolve never to miss an opportunity to say those three amazing words.

Of course, there are nonverbal ways to express your love, and they are at least as important as saying the words. In his book *The Five Love Languages,* Dr. Gary Chapman describes five "languages" with which to express your love to another person: words of encouragement, time spent together, physical touch, acts of service, and the giving of gifts. Everybody naturally "speaks" one or more of these languages. Just as importantly, everybody naturally "hears" one of these languages more than the others. In other words, everyone best receives love when it's expressed in his or her love language. Do you know the love languages of the people you love the most? It's important that you know how best to communicate your love for each of them.

You might assume that your family and friends know already how you feel about them. Almost certainly they do. Just the same, it's good for you to say—and good for them to hear. Love is the one reminder no one objects to receiving.

63

START TRAINING FOR A 10K RUN

You set goals. You create an action plan. You move, one step at a time, toward the fulfillment of your goals. That's what you've been doing your whole career. It's how you move on to the next level, how you stretch yourself to be better than you've been before. And that's exactly what you do when you decide to train for a race. Running a race isn't strictly a physical activity. It requires discipline, mental toughness, will power. When you train, you aren't just training your body. You're training your whole self to keep working toward goals, to stay sharp, and to not let laziness overtake you.

A 10K is a great race to work toward. At 6.21 miles, it's long enough to require a certain amount of training, but it's much more manageable than a marathon. You have to be in good shape to run that far, but you can get there without being obsessive about it or letting it take over your life. Your body is made to be pushed beyond its comfort zone. It thrives on a challenge, on short-term pain that leads to long-term gain.

Retirement obviously means more leisure time. But leisure doesn't mean vegetating or drifting aimlessly. If you want to keep mind and body sharp, you still need goals to work toward. Training for a 10K race is one way to do that. The rewards—a stronger body, a tougher mind, the satisfaction of a goal set and a goal met—are far better than a winner's medal.

64

CHECK OUT
THE COLOR
OF YOUR
PARACHUTE

T hink about your assets. They go well beyond your stocks, bonds, and real estate holdings. Some of your most important assets are carried in your head. The knowledge you've gained over the course of your career is one of your most important assets, and there may be ways that asset could continue to generate income even after you retire from your current job. Consulting, for example, is a great choice for a retiree.

Consider the benefits. You're still using your skills and knowledge regularly, but you aren't as embroiled in the day-to-day tedium of the office environment; and hopefully you're outside the reach of office politics. Ideally, consulting is a more concentrated version of your old job—all the challenging and interesting parts without all of the rest. You'd be surprised how many pointless meetings you don't get invited to when you're paid hourly consulting fees. And speaking of those fees! Consulting can be a lucrative enterprise.

Still another attractive benefit is variety. As an employee you are able to apply your work savvy only to the problems of your specific employer. But consulting would allow you to address and create solutions for interesting situations in a number of companies.

Consulting can be a nice transition between full-time work and retirement. But the framework for such a situation is best laid now, while you still have your foot in the game. Make it your business to find out which companies would be willing to pay for your knowledge once you're retired. Maybe your current company would hire you to do some of the same things you're doing now.

Retirement shouldn't mean simply drifting off into the sunset. Instead, it should mean an opportunity to continue to do your job—but this time on your own terms.

65

❧

START A BRAND-NEW FAMILY TRADITION

T hink back on your happiest memories. There's a good chance many of those are associated with family traditions—you know, like the weekend each year when you and all your cousins went camping with Grandma and Grandpa Peters. No parents allowed. Or the annual polar bear dip in Lake Michigan each winter with your brothers Tom and Chuck. Remember when your dog Scooter got spooked and knocked over the Christmas tree right in the middle of your Dad's dramatic rendering of the Christmas story? Dad never missed a beat, and you know that story by heart after all these years.

What traditions are you establishing for your family? If your answer is none, it's time to begin. After all, your children and grandchildren deserve memories too. Consider celebrating Christmas or Thanksgiving with the family at the beach or in the mountains. Meet at a certain national park for a family campout each summer. Or choose a day of the year—not an official holiday—and declare it a special day just for your family. Celebrate with a special meal and a little ceremony appropriate and unique to the event.

For example, institute "Family Cookie Day," when the women and girls in the family get together to bake Christmas cookies on the second Saturday in December. How about a summer pool party each year with prizes for most unique dive? A great idea might be Family Scrapbook Night: everybody brings pictures they've taken throughout the year—with extra copies if possible—and spend the evening documenting another year in your family's history.

You probably have ideas popping in your head already. Implement them. Let them work to draw your family together and keep it strong.

66

OBSERVE ARBOR DAY

A story is told of Marshall Lyautey of France, who instructed his gardener to plant a tree. The gardener objected, saying it would take a hundred years for the tree to grow to maturity. "In that case," said Marshall Lyautey, "there is no time to waste. Plant it this afternoon!" That's a great picture of a man who understands the big picture—a man who sees that it isn't all about him. To plant a tree is to have an eye to the future that goes even beyond your own life.

Think of the pleasure you get from a big, healthy tree. You enjoy looking at it; you stay cool in its shade; you listen to the songbirds that nest in its branches. Then there are the environmental benefits. Here's the thing to remember about a tree: if it's big enough to give you shade, there's a good chance you didn't put it there. That tree is a gift to you from someone who has gone before. You can say thank you by planting a tree that someday will be a pleasure to someone else.

Any kind of tree will do, but you might think about planting a nice slow-growing tree, such as an oak or an elm—one that will spread its leafy branches out to give shade and shelter birds long after you are gone. You might even think of it as a symbol of the overall good you bequeath to others as you go through life.

And here's a cool idea. If you plant a tree now, you might even be able to enjoy it yourself by the time you retire. At the very least, you'll be able to see it get a healthy start.

67

PERK UP
THE
PREMISES

E ver notice how things seem to fall apart all at once? You need a new roof the same year your furnace gives up the ghost. Storm damage comes along the same month your water heater springs a leak. You don't want to spend your retirement years—or your retirement dollars—making costly repairs or home improvements. Now might be the time for a home makeover. Spend some time and money now getting your house in tip-top shape so you won't have as much to deal with later.

You probably already have a good idea of how many years you have left on your roof and your furnace and air-conditioning unit. A good home inspector can give you advice on other areas of the house that might need some attention. And while you're at it, you might have a tree surgeon come out and assess the state of the trees in your yard. If you take care of your trees now, you can head off trouble later.

If you're fortunate enough not to need any major repairs, maybe you can take this opportunity to do some renovating. One of the kids' bedrooms could become a studio or a hobby room. A new porch might be just the thing for the new, more laid-back lifestyle you envision after retirement. You might need a new guest bedroom for visiting grandkids or missionaries on furlough. Think through what you want your life to look like after retirement and how your home might be more conducive to that lifestyle. After all, you're probably going to be spending more time around the house.

68

START KNOCKING OFF AT 5:oo SHARP

Punctuality has always been one of the great virtues of the American workplace. By being at your desk or on the work-site by 8:30 or 9:00—whatever time your shift starts—you communicate that you are committed to the work you do. Punctuality is a sign that you're willing to give full value to the people who sign your paycheck. It shows that you respect and value the time of the coworkers and clients who depend on you to be there for them every workday. Your punctuality communicates how seriously you take your responsibilities.

Has it ever occurred to you that leaving work on time is a kind of punctuality too? Your responsibilities go beyond the office. When you get home on time you communicate that you take your responsibilities at home just as seriously as you take your responsibilities at work. And the closer you get to retirement, the more your priorities should be shifting toward life beyond the office.

Think how many times you've called home to say you'd be working late. The message you're sending is, "Whatever is happening at work right now is more important than whatever I'm going to be missing at home." How many times over the course of your career have you sent that message? True, sometimes it can't be helped. Sometimes you're in the middle of something at work that truly is more important than getting home in time for dinner. But you are fast approaching a stage of life in which that will never be true again. It's time you started taking punctuality at the end of the workday as seriously as punctuality at the beginning of the work-day.

69

BECOME THE
CONSUMMATE
COLLECTOR

Y ou've heard the rumors. Folks retire, and then they start to collect things, like dozens of cats or porcelain unicorn figurines courtesy of the shopping network. Stop the insanity before it starts. Decide now if there is anything you have a genuine interest in collecting through the coming years.

If you already have a growing display of collectibles, take a fresh look at it. Ask yourself, "Do I really enjoy this or is it just a habit I've picked up along the way? Do I look at these items only when the dust grows so thick it becomes a health hazard? Does my collection add to the comfort of my home or does it add clutter I don't need?" Anytime your interest in a collection wanes, don't hold onto it out of sentimentality. Purge.

The difference between a pack rat and a philatelist (stamp collector), plangonologist (doll collector), or brandophilist (cigar band collector) is that the knowledge the folks with tongue-twisting names tend to have about what they collect is often larger than their collection itself. Retirement will offer you the perfect time to expand your mind along with your collection. So before you get there, carefully choose the direction you really want to go.

Becoming a consummate collector means becoming a discriminating collector. Focus on one or two specific types of objects to collect. Then learn all you can about them. This way, you can wisely appraise each addition, instead of picking up anything and everything that catches your eye. Continually evaluate both your finances and your available space as your collection grows. The more forethought you give to your collection, the greater appreciation you'll have for what is on your shelves.

70

BRIDGE THE
GENERATION
GAP

Y our days of "never trust anyone over thirty" have come and gone. Now it's your turn to be on the far end of the generation gap. It's easy to let this gap grow wider as you head toward retirement. After all, the younger generation seems so cocky and sure of itself. So sure that they know how to handle things better than you did. So sure that their music is more fun to listen to than the "oldies" station. So sure that "older folks" are boring. So much like you were when you were young!

It's true that every generation is a bit different from the last. But "different" does not imply better or worse. Differences can be viewed either as a barrier or as an opportunity to learn something new. Since health professionals have stated that learning something new is one way to keep your brain firing on all cylinders, why not go with the second option? Volunteer to spend time with people who are younger than you are.

This may sound like a backward idea. Young people should volunteer to help out the old folks. But there are plenty of "kids" in their teens, twenties, and even thirties, who could really use a few words of wisdom from someone who's on the flip side of say forty. But often what they need even more than advice is a parental figure who cares about where they are going in life, in their careers, in their relationship with God. Choose to be that person.

Ask those in the younger generation about their hopes and fears and dreams. Tell them how proud you are of their accomplishments. You'll find that friendship can bridge any generation gap.

71

━━━━━━━━━━━━━━━

TAKE THE
PLUNGE
INTO PET
OWNERSHIP

Having a pet can be demanding: finding time to attend to grooming, shots, exercise, finding a sitter when you leave town, even keeping those food and water dishes filled, or changing the kitty litter. And that's if you happen to have a low-maintenance pet. For most, it also means driving the neighborhood looking for them when they dig out from under the fence, or bolt out the front door every time a delivery person comes to the door, or simply wander too far from home. It means looking the other way when you find your best house slippers mauled or your sofa snagged. No matter how much you love them, bringing an animal into your home is work.

There is an upside to pet ownership, though. It's called companionship. Animals are able to give their owners a selfless and satisfying form of friendship. Sure you talk to them and they don't talk back, but most people consider that a plus. If you have taken a pass on pet ownership up until now, you might consider what advantages there would be to having a pet once you near retirement and have more time to invest in them.

Dogs, in particular, offer their owners an opportunity to stay active, a friend to go along on early morning walks or trips to the park. Cats offer quiet, unobtrusive comfort when the kids are grown and the house seems too big and empty. Birds are an almost constant form of beauty and entertainment. Fish can become an exciting hobby. All animals have something unique to add to the lives of their owners.

A pet can be a tremendous blessing in your life. You won't know just how much until you look into their eyes, listen to their chatter, or watch them peacefully glide across the fish tank.

72

SWING FROM THE MONKEY BARS—JUST TO PROVE YOU CAN

Remember the freedom of the playground? The bell rings and the whole school spills into the schoolyard. The swings soar back and forth, back and forth. "Higher! Higher!" A child reaches the top of the swing and leaps out in a high arc, landing in the grass in a run and tearing off to the merry-go-round, where the children whirl past—a blur, chanting "Faster! Faster!" to the children who give them a push before jumping on the merry-go-round themselves.

How long has it been since you have played with that kind of abandon? Maybe it's time you visited a playground and got in touch with your inner child. Remember what it was like to feel that free. Think how much good it would do you to climb on the monkey bars—just to prove that you still can. You're only as old as you feel, after all. Life can play tricks of perspective on you. You reach a point—probably before you even reach adulthood—where you think you're too mature to climb on the monkey bars. Then, somewhere along the way, you start believing you're too old to climb on the monkey bars. Are they beneath your dignity? Maybe so. But wouldn't you at least like to know that you can still tackle them?

What else do you feel too old for? What are those things that once gave you joy but now seem like a distant memory? Maybe you should make a list, then start checking them off—start finding out if you are really too old, or have you just let yourself drift away from some of those little things that used to make you happy?

73

CONSIDER
MOVING
NEARER YOUR
CHILDREN

No doubt you've already done some thinking about where you're going to live after you retire. When you're not going to the office five days a week, you may not have compelling reasons to stay where you are now. There are plenty of options open to you—Florida, Arizona, a house in the mountains, perhaps staying put. Have you given any serious thought to moving closer to your children and grandchildren?

Sometimes it feels as if life is making decisions about you rather than you making decisions about life. You may have moved around for your job; there's a good chance that's what brought you to the place you live now. But after you retire, you have the chance to decide where to live based on other concerns—based, for instance, on proximity to the people you love the most. Your grandchildren are only young once. And even though your adult children don't depend on you in the same ways they used to, they still need your love and support. What a blessing it could be to be more involved in their lives and to help them to bear their burdens. Babysitting alone could be a huge help—and it's so much more than babysitting when it's your own grandchildren that you're caring for.

Maybe Florida or Arizona is the right place for you after you retire. And there are certainly many fine retirement communities to choose from, all designed around the needs and interests of retirees like yourself. But you might want to check out a retirement community closer to your children and grandchildren. Imagine it— love, leisure, and convenience in one lovely package.

74

LEARN TO SAY YOU'RE SORRY

You clean out your desk. You tick off the last action items from your last meeting. You hand off your accounts to the person who will be your replacement. In many ways, retiring from your job is about tying up loose ends and closing accounts. You clear the decks in order to get a fresh start on the next phase of life.

When you apologize to another person, in a way you're doing the same thing. You retire the hurt you have caused. You tie up loose ends in a relationship, lest they trip you up later like untied laces on your tennis shoes. Anytime you apologize, you're closing old accounts—paying off a debt you have incurred in a relationship in order to get a fresh start with the person you have hurt.

If you are married, you and your spouse will probably be seeing more of each other after you retire. That means you'd better brush up on your relationship skills. You aren't going to have the option of going off to work instead of dealing with hurts and brokenness in your relationship. No, the two of you will be right there together, forty hours a week more than you used to be. That's a long time to seethe. That's why it's more important than ever for you to get good at saying you're sorry. And it's important to know when you need to say it—without being asked. Now is a good time to retire old hurts.

75

❧

BECOME A
FRIEND
OF GOD

Devotional time on the fly. Prayer on the wing. A forty-hour workweek can make spending time with God pretty difficult. It's worth it, of course—you know that. But won't it be wonderful when you can take all the time you want with God in the morning and still have energy to spend even more time with Him in the evening? When you can take a walk together in the afternoon and read His love letter to you—the Bible—slowly for greatest retention and understanding?

Once you are retired, you will have plenty of time to develop a strong, vigorous, friendship with God. You will be able to spend long periods of time just listening for His voice, studying His Word, ensuring that you understand His heart, revel in His love, and fulfill His every purpose.

Your life after retirement can be the most important, rich, productive time of your life. It can be a time for seeking the most important thing of all, reaching that one pinnacle that will burn strong even in eternity. Retirement can be spent in the most glorious pursuit on earth or in heaven—friendship with almighty God, your Savior and King.

Of course, you can't look at relationship with God as some chore you can better manage after retirement. Instead, it should be seen as a precious privilege that you attend to each day, no matter how busy you are—a privilege that will blossom and thrive once you are released from the tyranny of the urgent and able to give it your full, undivided attention.

76

PICNIC
UNDER
THE STARS

A blanket. A basket. A few sandwiches. A picnic is one of life's simpler pleasures. Awe inspiring? Maybe not.

But a picnic at night with the stars wheeling overhead—well, that may be awe-inspiring after all. Because the stars call you to reflect on your place in the vastness of the universe. They call you to consider a God who flung those millions of stars into place and keeps them all in their appointed paths—the same God who holds you in the palm of His hand. No, a starry sky is not the sort of thing to be taken lightly.

A picnic under the stars reminds you of something that is easy to forget: the life you live offers homey, simple pleasures like a picnic and the awe-inspiring grandeur of a sky full of stars, both at the same time. A sandwich eaten on a breezy hillside says, "What a good life that offers up its pleasures as easily as this," while the stars overhead take you outside of yourself and remind you that you are part of a much bigger plan. They remind you that you aren't the center of the universe—that it's not all about you.

That's an important thing to remember at any time of life, but especially as you contemplate retirement when you're tempted (even encouraged) to live entirely for yourself. A life well lived is a little bit like a picnic under the stars: You drink deeply of life's little pleasures and, all the while, you're reminded of the vastness and intricacy of the vast plan of which you are a part.

77

NAME
YOUR
NOVEL

Y ou've been dreaming about writing a novel for years. Your characters "talk" to you all the time. You hear them in the grocery store, at work, and every time you pick up a novel to read. Their stories are just waiting to be told, and you reassure them that in due time you'll do just that—but not while you're working forty-plus hours and handling all of your other responsibilities.

The time is coming when you will have time to tell the story that's in your head, but while you're waiting, give your dream a name. When you name something, you are legitimizing it, giving it life, strength, substance—not to mention that it can be a lot of fun.

Come up with a list of fifteen or twenty possible titles for your novel. Use some of the various techniques that your favorite authors use to determine a title. Use a play on words that captures the essence of your novel, use contrasting words ("Fire on Ice"), or write down the most unique word that might describe your sense of the work.

Try out the names—each one for a few days or weeks—canceling out the ones that don't work for you and adding new ones to the list. Ask a few friends out to lunch and march each title down the runway for them. (You might have to do this several times.) See how the titles look in written form or on the computer screen. Go around saying the title out loud and noting any responses you might get. When the right title comes along, it'll have a ring of truth, and you'll know it's the one.

One day you'll have all the time you need to bring depth and maturity to your novel. Until then, get busy naming your baby!

78

❧

INVEST IN
ETERNITY

Young people think that time will always be on their side. That they will always be strong and healthy and ready to tackle any challenge. Only when we have a few years under our belts do we see that we are all in decline—moving closer to the end with every breath we breathe, every minute we live. If this life is all there is, we will all come to the end of our days with disappointing results.

But, happily, there is more—a whole eternity more! What happens here on earth is merely a shadow of a fuller, richer life to come. All the more reason to look past our present limitations and invest in those things that last forever. Your career will come to an end, but the love you have bestowed on others will not. Your health and physical vigor will decline, but the strength and vitality of your spirit and soul will not. Your physical eyes will dim, but not your spiritual eyes. Your academic accomplishments will cease to matter, but not your acts of kindness and understanding. Faith in your own ability to conquer every obstacle will eventually disappoint you, but not your faith in God and His omnipotence.

As you approach retirement, begin to reprogram your thinking. Turn your focus to life after life, and make sure that you are investing in eternal realities. This is a better investment than the finest 401K. It trumps the most aggressive mutual fund. Get to know your heavenly Father, and you'll find that some of the greatest things in life can't be earned or paid for.

79

SIMPLIFY, SIMPLIFY, SIMPLIFY

Remember when you were just starting out? It was all about accumulating things—your first apartment, your first house, your first new car. Each item you purchased was a triumph. Slowly, but surely, you furnished your home and bought the things you needed for a rich, full life—maybe even some luxuries along the way. It was exciting. But as time went on, you may have realized that maintaining all that stuff was a big job, one that gets tougher every year.

Most people discover at some point in their lives that "less is more," realizing that they are working overtime to keep up with things that no longer add value to their lives. Do you really need two cars, a truck and trailer, a boat, and a motorcycle? You haven't even been out in the boat since Franz and Caroline visited from Germany. Do you need two sets of good china or will one set be perfectly adequate? Maybe it's time to pass along one set to a daughter or daughter-in-law. There is a splendid freedom in finding your comfort zone and divesting yourself of anything that doesn't fall within its boundaries. It gives life the feel of a good fit.

Don't wait until you retire to begin the process of simplifying. At that point, it will seem unwieldy and intimidating. Instead, start slowly by looking around, noticing what you use and what you don't use, what is too dear to part with and what you have no emotional attachment to. Balance that against the time and effort it takes to care for those items and who might be thrilled to take them off your hands. Ramping down can be just as much fun as ramping up— maybe even more!

80

❦

QUIT WORRYING
ABOUT WHAT
OTHER PEOPLE
THINK

I t's at its peak in the teen years. For the very young, it seems as if everything is about what other people think. *Do I fit in? Am I lacking in some area of physical appearance, personality, or fashion sense?* A few years later, most people find that they've traded those concerns for others. *Did the boss like my presentation? Do my coworkers respect me? Is my yard as nice as the neighbors'? Does my car send the right message?*

That self-questioning is pretty normal, but there should come a time in your life when the primary question begins to be—*what do I think about myself?* Rather than asking if you are meeting the expectations of others, you should be asking if you are meeting your own qualifications for a happy, successful life. That one particular is the hallmark of maturity.

Until you give yourself permission to overrule what others think, you will make no significant contributions to the world. Only when you quiet the external voices that rule you will you be able to hear and obey the inner voice that was designed by God to lead you to greatness. Only then will your life be your own, and only then will you be able to offer it to God without reservation. Now this is not about giving in to selfishness or being insensitive to the feelings of others. It isn't about shocking or offending others. It's simply about being true to yourself and to your Creator.

Take an inventory of your life. Are there things you deeply desire to accomplish? What's holding you back? If your answer is that you're worried about what others will think, worry no more.

81

START
RECORDING
THE FAMILY
STORIES

Have you ever noticed that the Bible is filled with stories, personal stories, in fact? God chose to help us better understand who we are by giving us glimpses into the real lives of real people. We learn about Adam and Eve and their sudden departure from the only home they had ever known. We learn about Abraham and his longing for a son. And there are so many others—Noah, Moses, Joshua, Samuel, Esther, Job, David, Ezekiel, the apostle Paul, Peter, James, and John, even Jesus. We know them through the stories.

Your family has stories as well. The story of how you met your spouse. The stories of your children's births. Stories of life-changing events, faith and courage, love lost and found. And there are stories that were passed down to you from those who went before. The story about Aunt Nessie, who helped to smuggle slaves from south to north right before the Civil War. The story of your father's brother Meryl, who was killed at Iwo Jima during World War II. What about the time your mother met Franklin Delano Roosevelt? There are stories all right. Lots of them. Poignant stories, humorous stories, touching stories. And they constitute your family's greatest treasure.

As time goes by, these stories can drop off the radar screen if they are not recorded and perpetuated by telling them to your children and grandchildren. Become the custodian of the family treasure. Get those stories down on paper or recorded on tape. After you retire, you'll have additional time to organize the stories, but begin to collect them now—before those who can tell them best have lost their voices.

82

OPERATE
FROM A
LOFTY POINT
OF VIEW

During the time you've been on the job, you have probably made the connection between success and positive thinking. No doubt about it, those who choose to look for the silver lining have a clear advantage over those who obsess about the negative.

The Bible, too, encourages an all-out positive point of view. Philippians 4:8 says it best: "Finally, brothers, whatever is true, whatever is noble, whatever is right, whatever is pure, whatever is lovely, whatever is admirable—if anything is excellent or praiseworthy—think about such things." Is your mind focused on admirable, excellent things?

As you approach retirement, staying positive becomes more critical for a number of reasons. First, a positive attitude promotes good physical and mental health. Constantly focusing on the failings of others, the disadvantages of your job, or the progress you haven't made can contribute to discouragement—even depression—while hampering your immune system, raising your blood pressure, and contributing to a variety of unhealthy conditions.

Second, a lofty point of view can promote strong relationships with others. When you think the best of others, they often sense it. And inspired by it, they become more cooperative, productive, and better team players.

Third, a positive perspective reduces the number of mistakes you make, sharpens your instincts, and gives you confidence.

Ditch the idea that if you aren't constantly thinking the worst or watching for errors, or suspicious of motives, you will be taken advantage of. Being positive doesn't make you dumb and blind. Instead, it focuses you on making the most of every opportunity and working smarter rather than harder. So look up. It's a God thing.

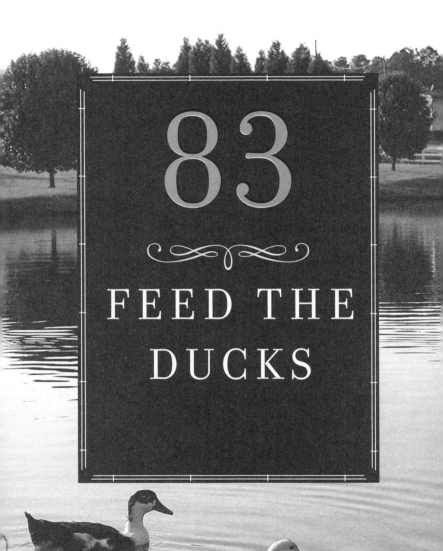

83

FEED THE
DUCKS

Sometimes it feels as if having fun is more work than going to work. Keeping the boat running takes a lot of effort and gobbles up a lot of money. Vacations are great, but between packing and unpacking and driving and dragging everything out to the beach and back, sometimes you find that you come home more exhausted than you were when you left. Every now and then you need to get back in touch with the quiet, low-maintenance, simple pleasures of life. In that case, all you need is a park bench, a bag of stale bread, and a pond full of ducks. It's very hard to beat duck feeding for return on your entertainment investment.

What's so gratifying about feeding the ducks at the park? It's hard to say, really. The ducks in a city park aren't much wilder than a lap poodle. Nevertheless, feeding them feels a little bit like getting in touch with nature without all the hassle of actually going out into the wild.

It's also fascinating to watch the group dynamics in a flock of ducks. The more aggressive ducks push the others out of the way to get closer to the bread. You can't resist throwing the crumbs directly to the weak and bashful of the flock. Even so, the alpha ducks tend to swoop in and try to get it all. While you're sitting there, think about the time when retirement will allow you to spend more time watching duck dynamics and no time watching office politics! Woohoo!

84

PUT A
NEW FACE
ON AN OLD
FEAR

I f you've ever jumped out of an airplane, you understand something all thrill seekers understand: Fear and exhilaration are two sides of the same coin. The exhilaration of hurtling through the sky is simply a controlled (or semi-controlled) version of the very legitimate and sensible fear of heights. Fear can be enslaving. It makes you shut down. But there's nothing more liberating than conquering your fears.

What are you afraid of? Think about those fears that cause you to freeze up and put unnecessary limits on yourself. Now think how you might face those fears directly. If you have a fear of heights, maybe you could try skydiving or mountain climbing. If the thought of public speaking causes you to break out in a cold sweat, you might join Toastmasters. If you suffer from stage fright, perform at a local restaurant's karaoke night.

Some fear is healthy; you *should* worry if the thought of jumping out of a plane doesn't scare you. So then, the key isn't so much conquering all your fear as conquering the irrational part of your fear. You do that by facing your fear in a controlled environment where you're actually safer than you feel.

Toastmasters is the perfect place to overcome a fear of public speaking because everybody is in the same boat, and you're safe from the ridicule that's your real fear. Skydiving feels incredibly dangerous, but you're actually quite safe in the care of your jumping instructor. When you face down your fear, you prove to yourself that you don't have to let irrational fear make decisions for you. So go ahead. Put a new face on an old fear, and turn fear into exhilaration.

85

MOONLIGHT
AT SOME-
THING
BRAND-NEW

Since the beginning, your career decisions have been constrained and limited by considerations of practicality. You've always kept one eye on job security, and the other eye on the career ladder. From time to time, perhaps, your passion and career pragmatism have coincided, and following your desires and interests has been a good career move. But those times were probably rare.

After you retire, however, you won't have the same constraints of practicality. If you aren't ready for a life of leisure, you can take a part-time job purely for the love of it. That is a serious luxury when you think about it. Are you a shutterbug? Get a job at a camera shop and spend the day chatting with people who share your interest in photography. Are you a bibliophile? Maybe you could take a part-time position at the library or at a bookstore. Sure, it wouldn't make sense to drop out midcareer and buy an ice cream truck, but that doesn't mean it doesn't make sense as you grow closer to a permanent vacation. Why not, if that's what you want to do?

You might also take a part-time job that doesn't pay. Here's your chance to follow your passion, and sometimes that doesn't carry any monetary reward. If you're retiring from the medical field, maybe you could volunteer at a free clinic in your city. Or you could volunteer to teach English as a second language to immigrants in your community. God has given you desires—He has given you the ability to make a difference in other people's lives. Start positioning now so that when you're free from the burden of practicality, you can make the most of it.

86

DEVELOP A
FONDNESS
FOR NAPPING

Have you tried rebooting?" That question is surely the first thing they teach in help-desk training. No matter what the problem with your computer, the person at the help desk always starts by asking you to reboot. And it's amazing how often the simple act of shutting down for a little while and starting all over again turns out to be all your poor computer needed. All that sluggishness, all that crankiness, all those bugs and tics sometimes go away with nothing more than a reboot. And suddenly the computer's actions are crisp and clean, as fresh as a daisy.

A little nap in the middle of the day is like a reboot for the human mind and body. It doesn't have to be a long nap either; in fact, long naps can sometimes be counterproductive, leaving you groggier than you were before. But a short little power nap of no more than forty-five minutes is like hitting your own reset button. You think more clearly. You're less prone to crankiness. Everything seems crisper, and you feel refreshed.

Very few work environments—in the United States, at least—lend themselves to afternoon naps. But you will soon be free to nap whenever you like. You might want to add napping to your daily routine. It's a great habit to get into. Don't think of a nap as lost time. Think of it instead as a way of maximizing the time that you're awake. A little siesta is like a mini-Sabbath in the middle of your day. It's a chance to recenter and rejuvenate, ready to come at life with renewed vigor. Have you tried rebooting?

87

GET A FULL-BODY CHECKUP!

When God first conceived of the human body, it was strong, perfect, and ageless. But Adam and Eve quickly put an end to that. Now we all have to deal with bodies worn down by living—an ache here, a pain there. Yowser! Who knew those once-nimble knees of yours would one day feel like two rusty fence gates.

There isn't much you can do about the ravages of time, but you certainly can maximize the quality of your time here on earth by staying healthy and fit. One of the most important components of that strategy is to get up close and personal with your family physician.

Even if you are relatively young and healthy, you should be in the habit of undergoing a complete physical exam once a year. This is especially important if you have a family history of life-threatening diseases. If you're over fifty, you should be checking in with your physician midyear, as well.

You might be surprised to learn just how helpful your doctor can be when it comes to getting the most out of your physical body. He can help you with sleep issues, arthritis, stomach problems—and not all by the use of drugs. Your doctor can help you make small changes in your diet that will pay significant dividends. He can introduce you to stretching techniques that will preserve your muscular function and exercises aimed at keeping your bones strong and your joints fluid.

You've been dreaming about all the things you want to do when you retire. Do your best during these crucial preretirement years to make sure you can enjoy postretirement to the fullest. The Bible calls your body God's temple. Let Him help you keep it a strong, healthy place to dwell—now and later.

88

DECK OUT YOUR TACKLE BOX

Babies have pacifiers. Toddlers have blankets. Teens have cell phones. And those in the working world have briefcases. It's kind of like a purse on steroids. It holds the lifeblood of your workweek—notes to self, to-do lists, important papers, "hot" projects, projects you've procrastinated on, day planners, magazines you don't have time to read, and probably a laptop with assorted technical doo-dads. As retirement approaches, it's time to loosen your grip on that briefcase and exchange it for the security blanket of retirement—a tackle box.

A tackle box is the briefcase of your future. It holds the promise of adventure, relaxation, and maybe even Friday night fish fries. If you already own a tackle box, chances are it rarely sees the light of day. Get it ready for its season in the sun. Fill it with hooks and lures and bait that would make any lackadaisical fish bite. Make sure your rod and reel are in tip-top shape. If you haven't tried fly-fishing yet, equip yourself for that, as well. Learning how to fly-fish is like learning how to dance with nature—without having to put on pointy shoes. Get out a state map and circle all of the spots where you hear the fishing is good. Then, "go fish."

If baiting hooks and handling flopping aquatic life is not your thing, there's still value in decking out your "tackle" box. Consider it a survival kit to help you "tackle" the upcoming gift of free time. Fill it with a book you'd like to read, crossword puzzles you'd like to complete, or letters you'd like to answer. What about a quilter's hoop, knitting needles, and thread? Then, head to that fishing hole anyway. To sit by the water, watch the sunlight play on the surface, and listen for the occasional fish breaking the silence of the afternoon with a flap of its fin is what enjoying the "good life" is all about.

89

DEVELOP
SIX-PACK
ABS

Over time, the force of chronological gravity (as well as a love of gravy) can transform six-pack abs into a proverbial keg—if you let it. Don't wait until you retire to look in the mirror and decide it's time to get in shape. The more healthy habits you acquire now, the better you'll look and feel when retirement rolls around. That means the better you'll be able to enjoy each and every moment of life. Why wait another day to begin?

You can get a good cardiovascular workout from walking regularly (or training to run that 10K!). But strength training is the secret to keeping your bones strong and your muscles toned. It also benefits your "core." That's the trunk of your body where all of your movement is centered. By strengthening your core, your center of gravity becomes more stable, resulting in better balance. You also strengthen your spine, which can help alleviate future back problems. In other words, strength training is not just for those who want Popeye-sized biceps or six-pack abs. It's for everyone who wants to stay active well into their retirement years.

Lifting dumbbells isn't the only way to achieve this goal. Try yoga or Pilates classes. Learn how to use an exercise ball. Even pumping soup cans can make a positive difference in your future. And don't ignore sit-ups and push-ups. They're still as effective as they were back in high school gym class—and they don't require any equipment other than your own stamina. Whatever routine you decide to try, be sure and check with your doctor before you begin. Then the only thing left to do is get started!

90

❦

EXCHANGE
THE BUSINESS
SECTION FOR
THE FUNNY
PAGES

You have a circle of friends who are ready to share a smile with you each and every morning—Dilbert, Hagar, Dennis, Marmaduke, Blondie, Rose, Calvin, Hobbs—just to name a few. Spending a few minutes with these "funny" friends is not only enjoyable, but it's good for your health. That's because laughter is good medicine. It can help lower blood pressure, reduce stress hormones, boost immune systems, increase muscle flexibility, and release natural pain-relieving endorphins—all without any potential side effects.

That's why exchanging the business section for the funny pages is a wise habit to acquire before you retire. The ups and downs of the stock exchange, as well as the careers of CEOs, may be newsworthy, but that doesn't make poring over them every morning worth your time. The funny pages may lower your blood pressure— but the business section has the potential to do the exact opposite. As a matter of fact, so does much of what you read in the morning paper.

Although knowing what's going on in the world is important, it's easy to overdose on the news. Either reading the paper or watching the nightly news is enough to fulfill that requirement each day. The human heart can hold only so many stories of crime and tragedy before it either becomes hardened or feels totally helpless. Anytime your heart reaches its limit, have a time-out with God. Turn the headlines into prayers for hope, help, and healing.

Then, remind yourself that joy and laughter is just as present in this world as sorrow and evil. Read the funny pages. It'll do your heart good.

91

MAKE A
DIFFERENCE
ON FOREIGN
SOIL

The world is often regarded as a retired person's playground—an exotic amusement park where you can see the sights and sample the cuisine, while picking up a few souvenirs and foreign phrases along the way. While there's nothing wrong with travel for travel's sake, in this day and age you have ample opportunities to turn your travels into something more. All it takes is a change of focus.

One thing retirement guarantees is plenty of "me" time. But constantly focusing on yourself can lead to tunnel vision. That's why expanding your horizons now is so important. When planning your vacation time this year, why not do something to change the world instead of simply taking snapshots of it?

You can choose to nurture a more accurate, and compassionate "world view" by volunteering on a church- or humanitarian-sponsored trip. Help build a church for a needy community or a home for an impoverished family. Pass out food at a refugee camp. Use your professional experience in the health care, business, or educational field. Even if the only skill you feel you have to offer is holding a child who feels all alone in the world, you can make a difference on foreign soil—in a way that will also make a difference in you.

To get an idea of the wide range of short-term projects available, visit the Web site for globalvolunteers.org or GlobeAware.org. Also, be sure to check with the mission board of your church or a local volunteer agency, such as the Red Cross, to see if they have any volunteer projects planned—expenses for many of these types of trips are often tax-deductible.

So, go ahead and see the world with new eyes. One person really can make a difference.

92

REPAY AN
OLD DEBT

Not every debt has a dollar amount. Some are accrued through kindness. But sometimes a debt of gratitude can feel harder to repay than a maxed-out credit card. A simple "thank you" seems so small, but it may be all you have to give at the time. Not that the person who gave you this gift of love expects anything in return. Generosity never gives to get. But that doesn't mean repaying an old debt isn't a good idea. Sometimes, it's God's way of answering prayer.

Think back over your life. Who came to your aid when you needed it most? Who helped you out physically, financially, or emotionally? Who stuck his or her neck out to help save yours? It may be a parent or family member. It may be a teacher, a pastor, a mentor, a counselor, a doctor, a police officer, an EMT, a fireman, a boss, a coworker, a neighbor, or a friend. It may even be a stranger.

Whoever these personal heroes may be, take a moment to thank God for bringing them into your life. Then, ask God if there is any way you can reciprocate for what was done for you in your past. The answer may be as simple, yet as heartfelt, as writing a letter or making a phone call. Or perhaps you could present that special someone with a memento honoring his or her selfless gift.

There is also the chance that the people who once filled a need in your life are now in need themselves. Ask around. See what you can find out about the struggles these individuals may be facing. Then, see if there is any way you can help them the way they helped you. And don't ignore the gift of prayer. Asking God to bless those who've been a blessing is a way to praise God and help others at the same time.

93

EXPLORE THE OUTER LIMITS— OF YOUR HOME- TOWN

Retirement can take you places. Like Florida. But you're not there yet. While it's wise to plan for the future, it's also wise to enjoy wherever it is you are today. The place you call "home" is not just a rest stop on the way to something else. It's where God has planted you for this season of your life. If you don't set down roots, you can't grow strong and tall. One way of encouraging those roots to go deep is to get to know where you live by exploring the outer limits of your hometown.

Get out a street map of the area where you live. Look it over. Search for parks you haven't visited or neighborhoods you've never seen. Look for lakes, landmarks, and old country roads. Then, pack up a picnic and take a drive.

On Sunday, study your local paper. If there's a new restaurant in town, give it a try. If a neighboring community is holding a garlic festival or Maypole celebration, get out and participate. Read anything you find about the history of your community. Look at old maps to get a picture of how it's grown. Talk to old-timers about what it was like before the freeways and fast-food restaurants moved in. Ask friends and neighbors about their favorite things to do in town on a free afternoon. Instead of taking your usual short-cuts, venture to take a long cut by exploring a street that's new to you.

Retirement can offer you a chance to explore the world. But for now, why not find contentment in a weekend at home, exploring the hidden treasures of your very own backyard.

94

WEAR YOUR
HEART ON
YOUR
SLEEVE

When you were a little kid, you laughed uncontrollably when the mood struck. You cried when your feelings were hurt. You loved your friends so much that you thought the world would end if they moved away. You found joy in simple things like ice-cream cones and fireflies. You sang even if you couldn't carry a tune. You danced even after the music ended. You believed in miracles, magic, and living happily ever after.

But somewhere along the road of life, kids learn to put a poker face on their emotional side. Maybe it's peer pressure. Maybe it's self-consciousness. Maybe it's simply trying to act "like a grown-up." Whatever the reasons, they're all behind you now. But that kid inside is still alive and well. Why not let him or her teach you a thing or two about getting the most out of life—beginning with getting real about how you feel.

Wearing your heart on your sleeve doesn't mean that you have to cry at every greeting card commercial or end every guy's poker night with a group hug and an "I love you, man." All it means is that you're fully connected with your emotional side and that you're not afraid to show it. If you want to see what emotional balance looks like in action, read the gospels. You'll see that Jesus never hides how He feels.

If you've allowed your feelings to go into retirement before you do, it's time to let them see the light of day. Say, "I love you," "I'll miss you," or "I'm proud of you" without hesitation. Ask for help when you need it. Compliment others when they deserve it. Whistle just because you feel like it. Dance with abandon. Sing with conviction. Let the tears fall and the laughter roll. Learn to live from the heart. If kids can do it, so can you.

95

❦

EXAGGERATE, EMBELLISH, & OVERSTATE

S ince toddlerhood, chances are you've used words each and every day. If conversation truly is an art, you'd assume that everyone who reaches retirement age would have enough practice to make them a certified master of chitchat and banter. Unfortunately, that's not always the case. For many people, what's up at work is the heart of almost all of their communication. The rest of their words are used to give and gather information, such as "Did you take the dog out for a walk?" or "I'll have the ham on rye." When basic communication replaces personal conversation, relationship pays the price.

Like your muscles, conversational skills can atrophy with disuse. But you can start whipping them into shape right now. Begin by learning how to tell a good joke. Take a mental note of jokes you hear or read in the paper that really tickle your funny bone. Then, try them out on others. Go ahead. Exaggerate, embellish, and overstate. Become a storyteller that compels others to listen—and then leaves them wanting more.

Telling jokes and stories can be a great icebreaker to get a conversation going. To keep it going, you need to involve those around you. Ask insightful questions. Listen without interrupting. Pay attention to what others are saying instead of rehearsing in your head what witty remark you'll interject next. If you truly care about those you're conversing with, you'll want to hear what they have to say.

The more of a master you become at the art of conversation, the less chance there will be of you becoming one of those retired folks who can only talk about "the good old days." Each brand-new day will hold enough good stories of its own just waiting to be shared.

96

❧

READ THE
OWNER'S
MANUAL

W hen you get a new car, it comes with an owner's manual. This important book holds all kinds of vital information about maintaining your shiny, new investment. It lets you know what type of fuel your car needs, what the warning lights on your dashboard mean, and how to use the "techno-gadgets" that come with your specific model. If you never glance at the owner's manual, you can still operate your car, but you'll miss out on enjoying its full potential. You may get fewer miles to the gallon because you didn't know your new turbo engine needed high-octane fuel. And you may never discover the really cool hidden compartment for your MP3 player.

Like your car, life has an Owner's Manual. Without reading it, you can get by day-to-day. You can go to work, build a family, and plan for your retirement. But if you take time to study its pages and apply what you've learned, you'll find life a much more fulfilling journey, both before and after retirement.

The Bible is God's Owner's Manual for life. Inside, you'll find tips on how to properly maintain your relationships, resources, and integrity. You'll learn about warning lights that can keep you from heading the wrong direction. You'll also uncover where to find peace, joy, and a life that never ends. In short, you'll discover how to fully live the abundant life God has planned for you.

Like your vehicle's owner's manual, the Bible is a bit over-whelming to read all in one sitting. Instead, read a chapter or two each day. Use the topical index to find help with specific challenges when they arise. Then take what God teaches you out for a spin. Applying what you learn is where the rubber truly meets the road.

97

TAKE UP GARDENING

Y ou don't need a garden to teach you that life is made up of seasons. All you have to do is look at your own personal journey. However, as you near retirement, looking back may make you long for seasons that have already passed instead of making you anticipate the new seasons to come. Taking up gardening is one way to keep you looking toward the future—to put the "spring" back into your step, so to speak.

Tending a garden gives the nurturer in you room to bloom (without the responsibility of having to adopt a puppy or give birth to another child!). As you till, plant, prune, fertilize, and water, you do more than "tend" a plot of land. You work hand in hand with God to cultivate a bona fide miracle called "growth." Every seedling that springs from the soil, every bulb that bursts to life after a long winter's chill, every piece of fruit that the sun ripens to sweetness is a reminder that growth is an ongoing process. Even when it appears nothing is happening, a lot is going on beneath the surface. The same is true with you.

So forget dusting silk. Pull up the weeds from that old flowerbed. Break out the seed catalogs. Visit a nursery. See what kinds of plants please your eye and thrive in your climate. Consider how much attention each type of plant needs and how much you are willing to give. If an herb garden on your windowsill is all you feel you can commit to, that's fine. Starting small is a great way to get your green thumb in shape. The season is coming when you will finally have time not only to stop and smell the roses, but to prune them too.

98

HOST A DESSERT BUFFET

An active social life can keep you feeling like a youngster, even if you've got an AARP card in your wallet. While you're still part of the working-for-a-living crowd, keeping socially active is fairly easy. You have coworkers to chat with during lunch breaks and at office Christmas parties. Even casual camaraderie in the parking lot can help keep you connected—feeling part of a world that's bigger than the four walls of your home.

After retirement, some people feel as though those walls are closing in. But they don't have to. Start now to focus on strengthening your connection with others, socially and relationally. One great way to do that is to host a dessert buffet. It's easy. It's interactive. And it involves extremely appealing things such as cheesecake, hot fudge, and pie a la mode. What's not to like?

Hosting a social get-together is as simple, or stressful, as you make it. Make up a guest list of people you'd like to know better. Invite coworkers, neighbors, or casual acquaintances. Don't worry if some of your guests can't make it. Ask them when would be a convenient time for you to schedule buffet number two!

Ask every guest to bring something to add to the buffet. It doesn't have to be fancy. You could host a make-your-own-sundae night where every guest brings a topping. Or ask guests to bring a bag of their favorite cookies. The key isn't to dazzle guests with your culinary expertise, but to get into the habit of being hospitable. The more at home you feel having others over, the more welcome others will feel in your home—and the easier it will be after retirement to have a strong social circle to keep you feeling young at heart.

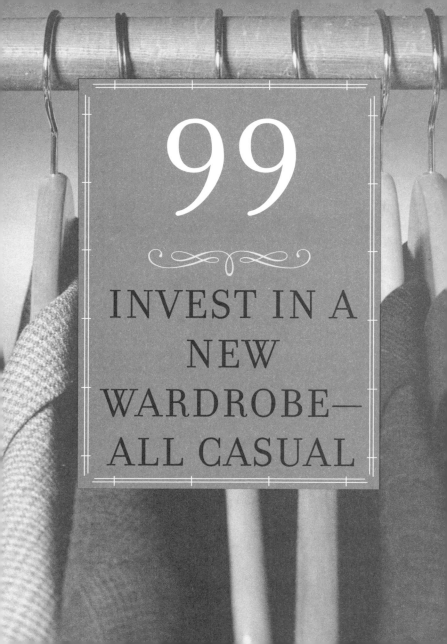

99

INVEST IN A NEW WARDROBE— ALL CASUAL

T he day is coming when panty hose and neckties will be a thing of the past. You'll exchange "business casual Fridays" for perpetual weekend wear. Instead of dressing for success, you'll write your own dress code, one where comfort, convenience, and self-expression dictate all the rules.

If you want to wear white before Labor Day, go for it. If leopard stretch pants, red chili necklaces, and gold lamé moccasins make your heart sing, here's your chance to make some beautiful music. If Hawaiian shirts, black socks, and leather sandals trip your trigger, you don't have to bite the bullet any longer. Your closet is under new management. Your inner fashionista is in charge. Yes, the kids may complain. Strangers may stare. Your spouse may roll his or her eyes when you don an outfit that's louder than a teenager with a new stereo system. But after retirement, why "dress to impress"?

Instead, dress to express who you are. Choose to wear what makes you feel confident, comfortable, and "put together" in your own way. Go for easy-care, wash-and-wear fabrics. Why spend money on dry cleaning when it could be better spent on greens' fees?

Before you retire, take a good look at your current wardrobe. Start to weed out your closet of business clothing you rarely wear. If you haven't worn something in over a year, chances are it has outlasted its usefulness. Don't let it just hang there gathering dust. Donate it to charity. Or take it to a consignment store where you can trade in your former fashions for your more casual future.

Then, take your new clothes out for a test ride. Practice for retirement on weekends. Wear whatever makes you smile.

100

CONSIDER
DOWNSIZING
YOUR
DWELLING

B e it ever so humble, there's no place like home." Is your home humble enough? It may be that you were in a very different place in life when you bought the house you now live in. You may have gone from several kids in the house to just you and your spouse, for instance. Perhaps you plan to spend a lot of time away from home after you retire, seeing the world, visiting grandchildren. Have you considered moving into a smaller place?

Lower energy bills, less maintenance, less housework—there are plenty of reasons smaller is better than bigger if you don't still need the space. Think how much less dusting you'd have to do or pay someone else to do. Fewer lightbulbs to change. A smaller roof to replace when that day comes. Then there's the equity you have in your house. Once you retire, you might be better off if that house equity were freed up to invest in mutual funds or bonds—some investment that would generate regular income. Your financial adviser can give you the lowdown on whether or not that makes sense for you.

Our culture tends to value the bigger over the smaller: If a fifteen-hundred-square-foot house is good, a three-thousand-square-foot house must be twice as good. And at this point in your life, maybe you can afford the bigger house with no problem. But is a bigger house really the best use of your money and resources? It's worth thinking about. Sometimes, less really is more.

101

SET THE
RECORD
STRAIGHT

I t may be hard to believe, but some people reach retirement age without really knowing who they are. Sure, they know their given names, what skills and talents they possess, and maybe even what brand of bean dip they enjoy the most. But a lot of people honestly believe they are someone other than who they are. A lot of people believe they are God.

This is identity theft on a grand scale. But it's easy to do. All it takes is building a life and planning a future that's centered on you, instead of around the one true God. However, impersonating a deity comes with hefty consequences. You never allow yourself the opportunity to mature into the amazing individual God created you to be. It's never too late to find out who that remarkable individual is.

When you believe that God is God—and that you are not—your life will show it. You'll hold more loosely to the things that are temporary in this life, like your plans and possessions. Your love for others, and even for yourself, will continue to grow stronger and more unconditional. And the clearer picture you get of who God is, the more you'll find yourself awed by Him.

So, set the record straight. Let go of the reigns of your life and accept the free gift of salvation that God offers you through His Son, Jesus. Receive Him and begin to discover how He will transform your immediate future, your long-term future, and your future beyond the trappings of this life.

THOUGHTS OF JOY FOR LIFE'S JOURNEY

Live your life each day as you would climb a mountain.
An occasional glance toward the summit keeps the goal in mind,
but many beautiful scenes are to be observed from each new vantage
point. Climb slowly, steadily, enjoying each passing moment;
and the view from the summit will serve as a fitting climax
for the journey

HAROLD B. MELCHART

Life begins at forty.

WILLIAM B. PITKIN

BEFORE I RETIRE,
I'D LIKE TO . . .

_____

_____

_____

_____

_____

_____

_____

_____

_____

_____

_____

_____

_____

_____

_____

_____

THOUGHTS OF JOY FOR LIFE'S JOURNEY

Independence: An achievement, not a bequest.
ELBERT HUBBARD

The best part of the art of living is to know how to grow old gracefully.
ERIC HOFFER

There is only one solution if age is not to be an absurd parody
of our former life, and that is to go on pursuing ends that
give our existence a meaning—devotion to individuals,
to groups or to causes, social, political, intellectual
or creative work.
SIMONE DE BEAUVOIR

BEFORE I RETIRE,
I'D LIKE TO . . .

THOUGHTS OF JOY FOR LIFE'S JOURNEY

The trouble with retirement is that you never get a day off.

ABE LEMONS
AMERICAN BASKETBALL COLLEGE COACH

Don't simply retire from something;
have something to retire to.

HARRY EMERSON FOSDICK
AMERICAN CLERGYMAN

Age is only a number, a cipher for the records.
A man can't retire his experience. He must use it.
Experience achieves more with less energy and time.

BERNARD M. BARUCH
FINANCIER AND ADVISER TO U. S. PRESIDENTS

BEFORE I RETIRE,
I'D LIKE TO . . .

THOUGHTS OF JOY FOR LIFE'S JOURNEY

Retirement at sixty-five is ridiculous.
When I was sixty-five, I still had pimples.

GEORGE BURNS
AMERICAN COMEDIAN

When you retire, think and act as if you were still working;
when you're still working, think and act a bit as if you were
already retired.

AUTHOR UNKNOWN

Preparation for old age should begin no later than one's teens.
A life which is empty of purpose until 65 will not suddenly become
filled on retirement.

DWIGHT L. MOODY
AMERICAN EVANGELIST

BEFORE I RETIRE,
I'D LIKE TO . . .

THOUGHTS OF JOY FOR LIFE'S JOURNEY

Man arrives as a novice at each age of his life.
NICOLAS CHAMFORT

At sixteen I was stupid, confused, insecure and indecisive.
At twenty-five I was wise, self-confident, prepossessing and assertive.
At forty-five I am stupid, confused, insecure, and indecisive.
Who would have supposed that maturity is only
a short break in adolescence?
JULES FEIFFER

At twenty years of age, the will reigns;
at thirty, the wit; and at forty, the judgement.
BENJAMIN FRANKLIN

BEFORE I RETIRE,
I'D LIKE TO . . .

_____

_____

_____

_____

_____

_____

_____

_____

_____

_____

_____

_____

_____

_____

_____

_____